Elijah's Mantle

Pilgrimage, Politics, and Proclamation

Elijah's Mantle

Pilgrimage, Politics, and Proclamation

Harold T. Lewis

A
JourneyBook ™
from
Church Publishing Incorporated New York

Cover art, "Elijah Fed by Ravens," courtesy of World Mission Collection, Wisconsin Evangelical Lutheran Synod. Used by permission.

Half-title page image is a detail of the rood screen from Calvary Episcopal Church, Pittsburgh. Photograph by Gateway Associated Photographers, Pittsburgh.

"O holy city, seen by John," words by Walter Russell Bowie. Used by permission of the Rev. Theodore H. Evans, Jr.

"Lord, you give the great commission," words: Jeffery Rowthorn © 1978. Hope Publishing Co., Carol Stream, IL 60188. Used by permission.

"We know that Christ is raised and dies no more," words by John Brownlow Geyer. Used by permission of the Rev. John B. Geyer.

"Father eternal, ruler of creation," words by Laurence Housman. Used by permission of Oxford University Press, New York, NY.

"O Love that wilt not let me go," words by George Matheson. Used by permission of Novello & Company Ltd., London, c/o Shawnee Press, Inc., Delaware Water Gap, PA.

"O God of earth and altar," words by Gilbert Keith Chesterton. Used by permission of Oxford University Press, New York, NY.

Library of Congress Cataloging-in-Publication Data

Lewis, Harold T.
Elijah's mantle : pilgrimage, politics, and proclamation / by Harold T. Lewis.
       p. cm. – (JourneyBook)
ISBN 0-89869-351-9 (pbk.)
  1. Lewis, Harold T. 2. Episcopal Church–United States–Clergy–Biography.
  3. Afro-American Episcopalians–Biography. I. Title. II. Series.

BX5995.L49 A3 2001
283'.092–dc21
[B]   00-065653

JourneyBook and colophon are registered trademarks of Church Publishing Incorporated

Church Publishing Incorporated
445 Fifth Avenue
New York, NY 10016
http://www.churchpublishing.org

5 4 3 2 1

God of the prophets, bless the prophets' sons;
Elijah's mantle o'er Elisha cast:
Each age its solemn task may claim but once;
Make each one nobler, stronger than the last.

Dennis Wortman, *The Hymnal 1940*, No. 220

•

Dedicated to
John Milton Coleman (1901–1961)
and
+Richard Beamon Martin
and
Percival Alan Rex McFarlane

•

Elijahs all
who lovingly cast their mantles
over this grateful Elisha

Preface

IN THE PAGES THAT FOLLOW, I have attempted to put together a series of meditations and reflections on (to use the words of my subtitle) Pilgrimage, Politics, and Proclamation. The first half of this volume chronicles my pilgrimage from "boatboy" to "cardinal rector," and since this section is largely autobiographical, I will refrain from saying a great deal more about myself here, except to comment that my Baptism fifty-three years ago was the beginning of a love affair with the church. The church was the center of my life. It was the institution that not only provided spiritual nurture, but inculcated in me a sense of pride and self-worth at a time when the world did not bestow on people of color a great deal of either. My family believed that "an idle mind is the devil's workshop," and saw church as the best place to thwart the devil's machinations. Church, be it for Sunday school, youth group, or Boy Scouts, was where you were when you were not at home, in school, or at piano lessons. In a world in which access to public amusements was limited and in which there was not a whole lot of discretionary family income, the church was the hub of our social lives. And it was also touted as the best possible place to find an acceptable spouse, which proved, in my case, more than conventional wisdom!

The second half of these reflections is comprised largely of excerpts from sermons and homilies I have delivered "at all times and in all places" during my ministry, and therefore fits into the "Proclamation" category. The first several of these are meditations on the church year. There is no "Politics" section. The inclusion of this word in the title refers to the fact that, as I have exercised my ministry in "this fragile earth, our island home," that ministry has been, of necessity, political—at times even fraught with political intrigue. This was nowhere more true than at the Episcopal Church Center in New York, where I worked for eleven years. Aware of this fact, and of my predilection to step into the fray and not avoid it, Frank Turner (recently retired Bishop Suffragan of Pennsylvania) admonished me: "You don't always have to have an opinion." Admittedly, I have not always followed my good friend's advice.

In my life and ministry, I have been inspired by the prophetic witness of Archbishop Desmond Tutu, who once quipped: "Anybody who says you shouldn't mix politics and religion has not been reading the same Bible I've been reading!" The advice of another archbishop has had a particular influence on my preaching. Donald Coggan, the late Archbishop of Canterbury, said once that a good sermon challenges the intellect, warms the heart, and motivates the will.

But what all these reflections have in common is that they take their titles from hymn texts. As a writer of hymns and a musician by avocation, I believe in the theology of hymnody, as well as the transforming power of music to bring us closer to God, to provide us with a foretaste of the heavenly Jerusalem. As a friend of mine used to say, "No one ever left church humming a sermon." I invite you to read, pray, and sing along with me.

H.T.L.
The Feast of St. Cyprian, Bishop and Martyr, 2000

"Take me to the water"

—Lift Every Voice and Sing II, No. 134

SOME YEARS AGO, during a sabbatical from my work at the Episcopal Church Center, I spent several weeks reading and lecturing at Codrington College, Barbados, the oldest Anglican seminary in the Western hemisphere. The trip was especially significant because Barbados is my ancestral home, whence all four of my grandparents migrated to the United States at the time of the First World War. One of the stories my family passed down is that my maternal grandparents, Edith and Harold (for whom I was named), met on a boat on which they were sailing from Bridgetown to New York. The vessel's lights had been extinguished to minimize the possibility of its being torpedoed, causing my grandparents to meet while groping in the dark!

During my visit to Barbados, the rector of St. Lucy Parish Church kindly allowed me to pore over old parish registers. And there it was—the Baptism of Edith Mildred, ten days after her birth on 30 September 1900, the last of the fourteen children of Joseph and Harriet Jordan. From the sacristy I made my way to the churchyard, where I discovered the weather-beaten tombstones of my great-grandparents. The whole thing was a tremendous *Roots*-like experience!

Edith Jordan and Harold FitzEustace Worrell married shortly after their arrival at Ellis Island. My paternal grandparents, Cyril and Miriam, came to the United States around the same time, and the Lewises and the Worrells settled within blocks of each other in brownstones in the Bedford-Stuyvesant section of Brooklyn. All four grandparents were present on a May afternoon in 1947, when my parents, Frank and Muriel, brought me to the font of St. Philip's Church in Brooklyn, where they had been married the previous year, and where my mother had been baptized and confirmed. The officiant was one of the parish curates, Charles Sedgwick, one of the many "sons in the ministry" of George Freeman Bragg, Jr.,

3

(distinguished historiographer of black Episcopalians and rector for nearly fifty years of St. James', Baltimore).

Both my Caribbean and Anglican roots are important to me. While a student at Yale Divinity School, I came into contact with black Baptists and Methodists who sometimes actually questioned my authenticity and integrity as a black man because I was a member of a "white church." Later, as a tutor at General Seminary, where I encountered (sometimes recently confirmed) white Episcopalians, I found that I was often expected to explain myself and provide justification for being an Episcopalian to people who found "black Episcopalian" something of an oxymoron. Such experiences actually provided me with the greatest motivation for writing the book, *Yet With a Steady Beat: The African American Struggle for Recognition in the Episcopal Church*, in which I attempted to explain why black people have remained in the Episcopal Church. In it, I point out that the West Indians' experience is unique in that they came from an Anglican church almost all of whose members were black, so that the idea that the Episcopal Church was a "white man's church" was entirely alien to them. But I hasten to add that, whether black Episcopalians' ancestors picked cotton on Southern plantations or harvested sugar cane on Caribbean plantations, they are among the most loyal, dedicated, and steadfast members of the church.

St. Philip's, Brooklyn, whose more than two thousand members gave it the distinction of being the largest parish in the Diocese of Long Island, was a congregation made up of both "strains" of black Episcopalians. It was into this loving and supportive community—as well as into "the congregation of Christ's flock"—that I was received through the sacrament of Baptism.

> *Take me to the water.*
> *Take me to the water.*
> *Take me to the water to be baptized.*
>
> Traditional Negro spiritual, "Take me to the water" *Lift Every Voice and Sing II*, No. 134

· · · · · ·

WE ALL WANTED to be like Freddie Dent. Freddie was the oldest (and tallest) of the three Dent brothers, and more often than not, he had the high privilege of leading the procession. He was thurifer. Vested in cassock, cotta, and white gloves, he wielded the brass thurible with such dignity and skill that we younger servers stood in awe. Body erect and left hand flat on his chest, he censed the nave, preparing the way for the crucifer and torchbearers, choir, clergy, and lesser altar boys at St. Philip's Church, Brooklyn. He had learned that his right arm, and more particularly, his wrist, did all the work. (Only inexperienced thurifers throw their whole body into the operation). An acolyte's debut was often at Freddie's left side as boatboy. We were taught that we were virtually an extension of his body. When he turned, we turned, or more precisely, pivoted, so that we were always at his left side, holding with both our little hands the incense boat, presenting it on demand to the celebrant who would take a few spoonfuls of incense from it to sprinkle over the charcoals.

Acolyting was serious business in those days. I think I excelled in liturgics at seminary because of what I learned from our acolyte wardens, Mr. Butler and Mr. Stewart. Practice was on Saturdays, and even for rehearsals, we donned our cassocks before entering the sanctuary. We learned the name of every vessel and vestment, and what its purpose was. If, for example, the priest needed an extra purificator and sent us to fetch one, nary an acolyte at St. Philip's would have to ask what a purificator was.

The rules for Sunday morning were imposed as much to instill discipline as to ensure that the liturgy proceeded "decently and in order." As an acolyte, you were to be in the sacristy, vested, fifteen minutes prior to the service. Only black shoes were tolerated, and they had to be shined. You remained on your feet and kept silent, which allowed you to be ready to fulfill any last-minute request from the clergy. At the altar, hands not holding anything were to be folded in front of yourself. If one hand was holding something, like a cruet or the priest's cope, the other immediately found its way to your chest. Eyes should be slightly downcast (which was code for "Don't stare at the girls' choir at 8:30 Mass"). A genuflection was defined as putting your right knee where your right foot used to be, while remaining perfectly erect. With regard to altar candles, etched into your mind was the rule that the "Gospel candle" (nearest the side whence the Gospel was read) never burns alone.

To this day, I remember (although I have no need of the information) how to hand a priest his biretta so that when he puts it on, the bladeless corner ends up on the left side of his head! On at least one occasion, I learned my lessons perhaps a little too well. Friars from the Society of St. Francis visited the parish for a weekend mission. They explained to us that the three knots on the cinctures of their habits stood for the three vows they had made when they were professed: poverty, chastity, and obedience. The next Sunday, I asked the rector what the one knot at the end of his cincture stood for. "That knot, Harold, stands for the end of the cord."

The sum total of all this was not to impart a whole bunch of facts, but rather a reverence for holy things. Church was special, set apart. It wasn't an extension of the playground, classroom, or living room. We were on holy ground, where the worship of Almighty God took place, and there was nothing else that happened during the week that was more important. Lessons like these last you for a lifetime.

> *Strengthen for service, Lord, the hands that holy things have taken;*
> *let ears that now have heard thy songs to clamor never waken.*
>
> *The feet that tread thy hallowed courts from light do thou not banish;*
> *the bodies by thy Body fed with thy new life replenish.*

Syriac Liturgy of Malabar; trans. Charles William Humphreys, "Strengthen for service, Lord," *The Hymnal 1982*, No. 312

"Like a mighty army moves the Church of God"

—The Hymnal 1940, No. 557

I GREW UP IN THE DIOCESE OF LONG ISLAND during the (admittedly waning) glory days of Anglo-Catholic triumphalism. Of course, I didn't know that at the time. It was just church. We were inheritors of the incarnational legacy of the catholic revival known as the Oxford Movement, which maintained that all the senses should be brought into play in the worship of Almighty God. Our eyes beheld magnificently appointed churches and beautiful vestments. Our ears were treated to glorious music and hymnody. Our nostrils were filled with the redolent fragrances of incense, and our tongues both touched and tasted the bread and wine which had become for us the Body and Blood of our Lord Jesus Christ. Intrinsic to the ethos of that era was a clear sense of authority, of pecking order. Father *did* know best, and bishops were seen as just "a little lower than the angels."

All of this came together once a year on Cathedral Day. The cathedral, after all, is the mother church of the diocese, and as in ancient times, the faithful were expected to make a pilgrimage to it. So from every church, from Montauk to Brooklyn Heights, in our island diocese—which had taken its motto from the Psalms, "I will set his dominion in the sea"— came busloads of Sunday school children, accompanied by their parents, their teachers, and their becassocked priests. We converged on Garden City, and spread our blankets on the acres of lawn that surrounded the Cathedral, and partook of our picnic lunches.

At the appointed hour, James Pernette De Wolfe, fourth Bishop of Long Island (affectionately known as "the last of the great prince prelates") would appear on the porch at the south entrance to the Cathedral. A portable throne had been set up, from which vantage point he could cast an episcopal eye on the hundreds of boys and girls who had come for the festival. Bishop De Wolfe was vested in a precious miter and glorious cope, which looked like they weighed a ton! His jewel-encrusted crosier was dutifully held at his side by his chaplain, a perpetual deacon (as we called them in those days) arrayed in a dalmatic. Then our father-in-God would examine us in the faith by reading questions from the Offices of Instruction. "What is your name?" A cacophonous babble ensued as each answered with the name given in Baptism. A barrage of other questions followed, but the one I remember most was, "What is your bounden duty as a member of the Church?" to which the answer was, "My bounden duty is to follow Christ, to worship God every Sunday in his church; and to work and pray and give for the spread of his kingdom."

When Bishop De Wolfe was convinced that we were sufficiently grounded in the faith, he rose, which, of course, was our signal to hit the deck! We knelt on the grass, heads bowed, and received his intoned pontifical blessing, which was broadcast by loudspeaker throughout the expansive grounds of the cathedral. And then the bishop led us all in a rousing rendition of "Onward Christian soldiers." (Perhaps Bishop De Wolfe knew that this hymn—often criticized for its alleged militarism—actually was written by a country curate to be sung as an outdoor children's procession on Whitsunday.) As we sang "Onward then, ye people, Join our happy throng," we marched happily, indeed, to the tables where our Sunday school teachers rewarded us with great scoops of ice cream! Cathedral Day taught me that with faith came responsibility. It taught me, too, that I was part of a great army of Christians, both in the church militant and in the church expectant. It also taught me that church was fun!

> Like a mighty army moves the Church of God;
> Brothers, we are treading where the saints have trod;
> We are not divided, all one body we,
> One in hope and doctrine, one in charity.
> Onward, Christian soldiers, marching as to war,
> With the cross of Jesus going on before!

Sabine Baring-Gould, "Onward, Christian soldiers," *The Hymnal 1940*, No. 557

"I shall not fear the battle, If thou art by my side"
—*The Hymnal 1982*, No. 655

THE VISITATION OF THE BISHOP for Confirmation was a very big deal at St. Philip's, Brooklyn. A space was reserved in front of the church for the episcopal limousine, and the churchwardens stood at the curb to wait attendance on our father-in-God. In the sacristy, the parish registers were set out for the bishop's inspection and signature. Acolytes' cottas were stiffly starched. Brass candlesticks, into which fresh beeswax candles would be inserted, were polished so that you could see your reflection in them. Owing to some obscure Anglo-Catholic custom the meaning of which now escapes me, a seventh candle was placed on the altar. On a table in the chancel next to the bishop's throne were arranged a lavabo and towel, with a piece of bread and a wedge of lemon. The purpose of the lemon was to remove the oil from the bishop's fingers after chrismation, and the bread was used to absorb the oil. (The chrism-soaked bread was later burned.)

There were normally forty or fifty confirmands, all about twelve or thirteen years of age. Confirmation took place at a younger age in those days, since it was then considered an "admission ticket" to communion. "And there shall none be admitted to the Holy Communion," read the old rubric, "until such time as he be confirmed, or ready and desirous to be confirmed." I distinctly remember the day that my godmother, taking seriously the promises she made on my behalf at Baptism, phoned my mother to remind her that "it's time to get the boy confirmed." Godmother would later give me a copy of the *St. Augustine's Prayer Book,* published by the Order of the Holy Cross, which "supplemented" the Book of Common Prayer with such things as an order of service for auricular confession, the Angelus, and even a few novenas!

Boys sat on the "Gospel" side, or left side of the nave as one faced the high altar (and the side from which the Gospel always was proclaimed in those days); girls sat on the "Epistle" side whence the Epistle was read (the right side as one faced the high altar). Our line-up of dark suits on the Gospel side looked somber in contrast to the profusion of satin, organza, and silk on the Epistle side. The girls in their white dresses and white gloves sat demurely in anticipation of the rite. But their crown and glory, literally, were the white veils they wore, the netting cascading over tresses that had been subjected to hot curling irons the night before. There was a faithful army of women in the parish part of whose ministry was to lovingly make, repair, and fit those veils year after year. We were to be commissioned, and we were in uniform. It was a serious rite of passage. Each of us went up to kneel before the bishop "severally," which in rubric-ese meant "one at a time." "Serial confirmation" along a communion rail—a timesaving practice that has developed in recent years—was never even thought of! Hands were laid on us. The bishop's oily thumb traced the sign of the cross on every forehead, and each of us was smacked on the cheek, a practice that had its origins in the rite used for the commissioning of Roman soldiers. After the last one was "defended with God's heavenly grace," we lustily sang "O Jesus, I have promised."

The Confirmation service was the culmination of several months of rigorous preparation. Every Saturday morning we presented ourselves in the parish hall, where John Milton Coleman, second rector of St. Philip's, taught us about Scripture, the Prayer Book, and even stewardship. During our last session, we were given our own numbered boxes of little pledge envelopes and instructed to bring our own offerings, however meager, to church every Sunday. Confirmation meant, among other things, that we had to make our own financial commitment, separate and distinct from the one made by our parents. I was a member of the class of 1960, the last to be taught the faith by Father Coleman. He died early in the following January, in the twenty-eighth year of his rectorship. He was a man who commanded the respect of his congregation and also of the community beyond the walls of the parish.

I remember how proud parishioners were that he was the first Negro to sit on New York City's Board of Education.

It is significant, perhaps, that the only things, apart from the importance of making a financial commitment to the church, that I remember from Father Coleman's class were two definitions. The first is that a parable is an earthly story with a heavenly meaning. The second is that a sacrament is the outward and visible sign of an inward and spiritual grace. The "Good Book" and the Prayer Book. Word and sacrament. Holding both of these in tandem has ever been at the heart of the Anglican ethos. I thought of that, eleven years later, when William Carl Frey ordained me to the priesthood with the words, "And be thou a faithful Dispenser of the Word of God, and of his holy Sacraments."

> *O Jesus, I have promised*
> *to serve thee to the end;*
> *be thou forever near me,*
> *my Master and my friend;*
> *I shall not fear the battle,*
> *if thou art by my side,*
> *nor wander from the pathway,*
> *if thou wilt be my guide.*

John Ernest Bode, "O Jesus, I have promised," *The Hymnal 1982*, No. 655

. . . . .

"Elijah's mantle o'er Elisha cast"

—The Hymnal 1940, No. 220

ON A TYPICAL SUNDAY MORNING at St. Philip's, Brooklyn, in the early sixties, I would take off my acolyte vestments after the 8:30 Mass and rush to the gym to help fellow members of the Young People's Fellowship (YPF) serve breakfast. Every week, between the 8:30 and 11:00 services, we offered parishioners bacon and eggs, hash browns, and toast for a dollar and a quarter, the proceeds being earmarked for the YPF's programs. Of those in attendance, there were usually three customers who didn't pay. They were the parish clergy, who arrived, at the stroke of ten o'clock, in cassocks and birettas.

One Sunday morning during breakfast, one of the curates, Alan McFarlane, approached me, out of the blue, to ask me what I wanted to do when I grew up. I told him I wanted to be an interpreter at the U.N. Then he casually asked me if I had ever thought of the priesthood. My response was to let out an uproarious laugh which caused some of our breakfasters to stop eating. When I gained my composure, I blurted out, "Father, I'm not cut out for that type of thing." Undaunted, Father "Mac" replied, "Harold, God does not choose the worthy, he makes worthy those whom he chooses." He was serious as a heart attack. I was speechless.

Part II of the conversation took place two weeks later. During the interim I had pondered all these things in my heart, but was still not convinced that God called garden-variety, horny adolescents to be priests. Our clergy were revered, in the words of St. Paul, as "vessels unto honor, sanctified, and meet for the master's use" (2 Timothy 2:21 KJV). I pleaded my sacristy-rat status, owning that I was "into" bells and smells—in other words, caught up in the externals of worship and not in its deeper spiritual significance—and I opined that *that* would be the wrong reason to seek holy orders. "Perhaps that is God's way of making

. . . . . .

12

it attractive to you," Father Mac offered in rebuttal. Part III took place some months later, after not a few sleepless nights. I had run out of excuses, and told the recruiter for Jesus that perhaps I might consider a priestly vocation after all. "Are you sure?" he countered. It seemed an unfair comment from someone who, I thought, should have shouted "Hallelujah!" when he heard the news. Then he added, "You should only go into the priesthood if you can do nothing else." By that he didn't mean literally incapable of earning a living in some other way, like teaching, medicine, or even interpreting. He meant that you should feel so compelled to do it that nothing else would fulfill you in the same way. Part IV of the conversation happened about two years later, after my first semester at college, when I could say, "Here I am, Lord, send me." I believed I was ready, in the words of the bishop's charge in the old Ordinal, to "dedicate myself wholly to this one thing."

We should always be praying, both privately and corporately, for vocations to the ordained ministry. Moreover, we should mention it, *en passant*, to young men and women at the time they are giving serious consideration to career choices. If we don't put the bug in their ears, they might believe themselves unworthy unless some Damascus Road experience befalls them. We must assure them that God does not always go the dramatic route.

> *God of the prophets, bless the prophets' sons;*
> *Elijah's mantle o'er Elisha cast:*
> *Each age its solemn task may claim but once;*
> *Make each one nobler, stronger than the last.*

Denis Wortman, "God of the prophets," *The Hymnal 1940*, No. 220

. . . . .

13

"I am thine, O Lord, I have heard thy voice"

—*Lift Every Voice and Sing II*, No. 129

RECRUITED BY FATHER MAC, endorsed by rector and vestry, approved by my bishop, I took the train to New Haven to present myself for an interview at the Berkeley Divinity School at Yale. This is where I would submit myself to what we unabashedly called in those days "priestly formation." This is where I would learn priestcraft—how to properly sing a proper preface, how to hold a baby at the font, how to hear confessions. This is where I would learn Greek and liturgics, Bible and church history, homiletics and pastoral theology. This is the school that one day would confer upon me the degree of *Divinitatis Doctor, honoris causa.* But for now, I was a twenty-year-old postulant for holy orders, believing, as we all did, that if only I could get a collar around my neck, I could save the world. I was wide-eyed and idealistic.

I was ushered into a room to meet a professor who was a member of the admissions committee. The Reverend Harry Jones lit a cigarette and, after a few pleasantries, asked me a question: "Mr. Lewis, did it ever occur to you that the Episcopal Church doesn't particularly like you?" I was incredulous, shocked. Although I understood from the context of our conversation that this was a reference to race, I still didn't understand. Black clergy had been my role models, and had encouraged me to follow in their footsteps. Several of the 2,000 African American parishioners at St. Philip's had patted me on the head when I was a boatboy, expressing the fond wish that I would be a priest. And so far as I could ascertain, *they* all liked me! The Episcopal Church was for me a black experience, and the only white Episcopalian I had ever seen in my home parish was the bishop. I was ignorant of church history. I didn't know that Absalom Jones, the first black priest, was ordained with the stipulation that his parish (St. Thomas', Philadelphia) not seek membership in the Diocese of

Pennsylvania. I was oblivious to the fact that the Episcopal Church's clergy were deployed along racial lines. I didn't know that my rector, Richard Martin (who would later become Bishop Suffragan of Long Island), had once been Archdeacon for Colored Work in the Diocese of Southern Virginia. Harry Jones knew I didn't know and was giving me, as I came to understand later, a reality check. Knowing that I would integrate the class of 1971, he wanted to prepare me for any incidents that I might encounter—and there were a few.

Harry Jones's reality check helped me to understand that the church, although holy, is made up of ordinary human beings. It is, as St. Augustine of Hippo is reputed to have remarked, not a hotel for saints, but a hospital for sinners. I didn't know that I would be called upon in my ministry to be a racial reconciler, or that I'd write a history of black Episcopalians. I was simply responding to a call to be a priest in Christ's Holy Catholic Church, not knowing where that call would lead me.

> *I am thine, O Lord, I have heard thy voice,*
> *And it told thy love to me;*
> *But I long to rise in the arms of faith,*
> *And be closer drawn to thee.*

> *Consecrate me now to thy service, Lord,*
> *By the pow'r of grace divine;*
> *Let my soul look up with a steadfast hope,*
> *And my will be lost in thine.*

Fanny J. Crosby, "Draw me nearer, nearer blessed Lord," *Lift Every Voice and Sing II*, No. 129

· · · · · ·

"Just as I am, thy love unknown has broken every barrier down"

—*The Hymnal 1982*, No. 693

I FOUND MYSELF one Shrove Tuesday in one of the massive oak confessionals in Christ Church, New Haven. (Our preoccupation with pancakes can make us forget that Shrove Tuesday takes its name from the verb "shrive," to forgive, and that traditionally many make their confessions on Shrove Tuesday in preparation for Lent.) I had entered the confessional knowing that the saintly Father Kibitz would be on the other side of the grille. To my opening line, "Bless me, Father, for I have sinned"—after which I indicated how long it had been since my last visit to the "box"—came the familiar response, "The Lord be in your heart and upon your lips that you may worthily confess all your sins." Then I took a deep breath and unraveled my laundry list of transgressions.

When I had completed this excruciating task, there was a very brief pause, which nevertheless felt like an eternity. I expected, I supposed, to be rebuked, chided, even castigated, but the confessor's words suggested none of these. He simply said, "It all boils down to the sin of pride, doesn't it?" My initial thought was that it was a cop-out response, and that Father Kibitz had dozed off and then said the first thing that had come into his mind when he realized I had finished. But as I performed my penance and pondered those words, I began to appreciate their validity. If the definition of sin is choosing to do one's own will and not God's, then the pithy, priestly remark rings true; it all boils down to the sin of pride.

Consider the parable in the eighteenth chapter of Luke about the Pharisee and the tax collector who went to the temple to pray. The Pharisee is a character who epitomizes the sin of pride. On the face of it, he was exemplary. He fasted twice a week instead of once a year; he gave a tithe on his entire net worth, and not just his crops. He was neither a thief

. . . . . .

nor an adulterer and took delight in contrasting himself with the tax collector in the parable, a man despised because he was recruited by the Roman government to exact taxes from his own people, and who, in all likelihood, skimmed his "commission" off the top. But the Pharisee discovers to his utter amazement, that despite all his outwardly righteous deeds, his prideful attitude made it impossible for him to accrue to himself any heavenly merit. It was, instead, the self-effacing tax collector who "stood afar off" who was found worthy. We would all like to say that we identify with the penitent publican, but if honesty prevails, we know that there is more than a streak of the self-righteous Pharisee in all of us. I told my Bible study group once that my own delusions of grandeur (read "absence of sufficient doses of humility") can be traced to at least two factors: 1) I was an only child; and 2) only one month after my ordination to the priesthood I found myself elected president of the standing committee in the Missionary Diocese of Honduras—which made *me* the ecclesiastical authority (given that our bishop had been forced into exile in the United States because of his outspoken criticism of the totalitarian regime in neighboring Guatemala). Ah, "pride cometh before the fall." We should probably recite daily the punch line from the parable: "Everyone who exalts himself will be humbled, but he who humbles himself will be exalted."

> *Just as I am, thou wilt receive,*
> *wilt welcome, pardon, cleanse, relieve,*
> *because they promise I believe,*
> *O Lamb of God, I come, I come.*

> *Just as I am, thy love unknown*
> *has broken every barrier down;*
> *now to be thine, yea, thine alone,*
> *O Lamb of God, I come, I come.*

Charlotte Elliott, "Just as I am without one plea," *The Hymnal 1982*, No. 693

· · · · · ·

"In his hand he gently bears us"

—*The Hymnal 1982,* No. 410

I HAD SPENT SO MUCH TIME in the months preceding our wedding, looking after myriad details—logistical, canonical, liturgical, and social, that my seminary classmates began to refer to my upcoming marriage to Claudette Nathalie Richards as "The February Follies." Claudette was living in Brooklyn, I was in New Haven, and the wedding was to take place in the Cathedral Church of the Incarnation, Garden City, Long Island. This meant that most arrangements—and reports of meetings with florists, caterers, and musicians had to be done by long distance telephone, and through occasional forays across Long Island Sound to and from Connecticut. I had procured permission from the Dean and faculty of Berkeley to "marry in course." Hugh Knight, the organist of my home parish, St. Philip's, was engaged to provide the music. Alan McFarlane, my mentor, flew in from Montreal to be deacon; one of my classmates was subdeacon. Other classmates made up the complement of acolytes and choristers.

Came the gelid (but mercifully snowless) day in February, and the sixty-five-minute ceremony, a pontifical nuptial mass presided over by my beloved father-in-God, Jonathan Goodhue Sherman, fifth Bishop of Long Island, went off without a hitch. A few details of the service are embedded in my memory. The first was the "the case of the missing collect." The books I had consulted provided for the reading of the collect of the day in addition to the nuptial collect. Since our wedding took place on the last Saturday before Lent, the collect would have been that for Sexagesima, which began, "O Lord, who seest that we put not our trust in anything that we do." I thought that was a bad omen and opted for a single collect. Another detail was the interminable gradual psalm. As the thurifer was swinging the thurible, creating great "wreaths of incense cloud" in anticipation of the Gospel, the plainsong

· · · · · ·

choir was intoning "Thy wife shall be as the fruitful vine upon the walls of thy house; thy children like the olive branches round about thy table, alleluia, alleluia," my soon-to-be wife and mother of our son turned to me and whispered "When will this be over?" Another detail was the rather pretentious rubric I had prepared for the bulletin which explained the rather pretentious practice of a non-communicating mass. It read: "During the singing of Bruckner's *Ave Maria,* the bridal couple will be communicated. The faithful may kneel." And the other thing I remember was Bishop Sherman, as he wrapped his cloth of-gold stole around our hands, proclaiming to all the world in his *basso profundo,* "Those whom God hath joined together, let no man put asunder."

But there was another detail of the service which escaped my notice then, but which, in later, politically correct days, raised my eyebrows somewhat—and that was the Epistle. While the 1979 Prayer Book provides a smorgasbord of lessons from which to choose, the 1928 Prayer Book offered a Hobson's choice for the Epistle: Ephesians 5:21–32, which contains the verse, "Wives submit yourselves to your husbands as to the Lord." All of us who have been sensitized to gender issues are tempted to dismiss this Pauline dictum as a culturally conditioned admonition, totally irrelevant to and out of sync with our modern understanding of gender equality and the dignity of women. Such an interpretation, I have come to understand, constitutes a rush to judgment.

Unfortunately, those who object to the verse do not take the trouble to read what precedes or follows it. The passage begins "Submit yourselves *one to another* out of reverence for Christ," and then goes on to make even greater demands upon husbands: "Husbands, love your wives, as Christ loved the Church and *gave himself up for her.*" For the writer of Ephesians to suggest, in a era in which women were chattel, that men love their wives as much as their own bodies, is radical, indeed. I believe that the reason Paul's words may offend us is that we have bought into a specious concept of equality and parity between the sexes. In a justifiable and well-intentioned attempt to redress the injustices of the vestiges of patriarchalism in our own society, we have erected in its place a tit-for-tat idea of equality measured by the number of meals cooked, the number of bags of trash taken out, the number of hours spent in child care, or the number of dollars earned. Couples who use calculators to measure the worth of their marriages are on very thin ice!

The *mutual* submission of which Paul speaks does not mean for a moment that one party becomes a doormat, a mindless, vapid creature who puts up with anything that mate hands down, including abuse. Mutual submission, rather, is that giving and taking, that art of compromise, that sacrifice, that ability to listen to the other party's concerns. Mutual submission presupposes the willingness to be vulnerable, the willingness to share pain as well as joy, adversity as well as prosperity. Equality in marriage is best achieved if we look at it as we do our investment portfolios—for overall performance over time, as opposed to judging it by the fact that it may have done miserably at the closing bell on a particular day.

At the tender age of twenty-two, my theology of holy matrimony was not so well developed. But I knew intuitively that, for our love for each other to be nurtured and sustained, Claudette and I needed, above all things, the blessing, guidance, and succor of Almighty God every day of our married lives. That is perhaps why we chose the following hymn for our wedding processional (and then chose it again in 1995, when Bishop Richard Martin renewed our vows at a Mass in the same cathedral offered by Orris George Walker, seventh Bishop of Long Island, in thanksgiving for our silver anniversary):

> *Father-like he tends and spares us; well our feeble frame he knows;*
> *in his hands he gently bears us, rescues us from all our foes.*
> *Alleluia! Alleluia! Widely yet his mercy flows.*
>
> Henry Francis Lyte, "Praise my soul the King of Heaven," *The Hymnal 1982*, No. 410

· · · · ·

"By schisms rent asunder, by heresies distressed"

The Hymnal 1982, No. 525

EVERY YEAR, during Christmas vacation, seminarians from the Diocese of Long Island were summoned by our bishop to a day-long retreat in Garden City. There was worship, there was lunch, and there was banter among the ordinands. But the foci of the day's activities were Bishop Sherman's addresses, delivered, *ex cathedra*, in the Chapel of the Mercer School of Theology. One day, the bishop expatiated on the church's ancient heresies and the councils convened to refute them. His erudite talk (he was, after all, a classics major, Yale, '29) was challenged by one of my fellow seminarians. "Bishop," he said, "why do we have to learn about all those ancient heresies? These are the sixties!" Without so much as batting an episcopal eyelash, the bishop responded, "We must learn about those ancient heresies, sir, because they are still alive and well in the church today." I thought about those words when two American priests were consecrated, in an irregular, and some believe, illegal service, in Singapore, and were sent back to the United States, purportedly to serve as missionary bishops to Episcopalians, or at least to some Episcopalians. A quick look at *The Oxford Dictionary of the Christian Church* confirmed my suspicion that those events were reminiscent of the Donatist controversy in the fourth century. The Donatists were a schismatic group who believed that the validity of the sacraments depended upon the moral worthiness and right actions of the ministers performing them. In 311, adherents in Carthage refused to recognize their new bishop because he had been consecrated by a neighboring bishop whose actions during the Diocletian persecution fell short of their rigorist ideals (they believed he had acceded to the emperor's edict and turned over his diocese's Bibles for burning). A rival bishop was consecrated, and the Donatists declared themselves the one, true Church.

In the second chapter of Mark's Gospel, a paralytic is brought to Jesus, but his friends can't get through the door of the house because of the crowds that had gathered outside. So they devise an ingenious "Plan B." They go up on the roof, cut a hole in it, and lower the man through it. Jesus, moved by their faith, first makes a *diagnosis* of paralysis—the utter helplessness of this man dramatically brought into his presence. Then he performs a *cure*: by his word alone, he forgives the man of his sins and heals him. And then there is a *manifestation* of Jesus' healing gifts, as the man picks up his pallet, and walks away. Then there is what exegetes call the "choric ending"—the response of amazement and renewed faith of the onlookers.

Controversial events in the church's life, with which the church becomes absorbed, even obsessed—be they irregular ordinations, Prayer Book revision, or the endless debate over human sexuality—render the church as paralyzed as the hapless man in the Gospel, a paralysis that impedes the church from carrying out the mission to which she has been called. Like the stalwart friends of the paralytic, we must bring the paralyzed and sinful church back to Jesus to be *cured* by him, even if it takes extraordinary means to do so. We must make our way through the gawking crowds who are delighted when the church engages in infighting. We must be about the serious business of cutting away the hardness of heart, the intolerance, hypocrisy, exclusivity, and holier-than-thou-ness that keep us from bringing about the wholeness and unity for the church that is Jesus' will. Then can we demonstrate our oneness with him and with one another by picking up our pallet, and walking out on our own steam. And the crowds, like those who witnessed the miracle at Capernaum, will be amazed.

> *Though with a scornful wonder men see her sore oppressed,*
> *by schisms rent asunder, by heresies distressed;*
> *yet saints their watch are keeping, their cry goes up, "How long?"*
> *and soon the night of weeping shall be the morn of song.*
>
> Samuel John Stone, "The Church's one foundation," *The Hymnal 1982*, No. 525

"In street and shop and tenement"

—The Hymnal 1982, No. 582

BEFORE THE ADVENT of standardized General Ordination Examinations approved by the General Convention in 1970 and first given in 1972, each diocese administered canonical examinations which had to be passed before the bishop would lay hands on you. I remember well the routine in the Diocese of Long Island. The examining chaplains gave each candidate five dollars for every exam taken, which, in those days, would cover lunch and roundtrip fare to Garden City on the Long Island Rail Road. But if you failed one of the exams, the five dollars was not given for the retake! I have an especially vivid memory of my examination in Holy Scripture. I was loaded for bear! On the tip of my tongue was a well-thought-out solution to the "Synoptic Problem." I was ready to expatiate on the doctrine of the High Priesthood of Jesus Christ as developed in the Epistle to the Hebrews. And as for theories of authorship of the Pentateuch, my seminary education had given me a bellyful of the Jahwist, Eloist, Deuteronomic, and Priestly sources (or J, E, D, and P, as most scholars reference them), which meant that anything having to do with Old Testament "alphabet soup" was going to be—if I may mix my metaphors—a piece of cake! I was not prepared, however, for the examiners' final question : "Mr. Lewis," said Father Wright (who was later to become Bishop Suffragan of New York) in his most inquisitorial tone, "It is said that the Bible begins in a garden and ends in a city. Comment on the role of the city in Holy Scripture." I was flabbergasted. But in my mind's eye, I scanned Holy Writ from Genesis to Revelation, trying a) to remember the name of every city mentioned therein; and b) to think of something half-way intelligent to say about each of them.

There is a lot of talk nowadays about "urban ministry." It has become a buzzword. "Urban ministry" is a *retronym*, a word which—according to William Safire of *The New York Times*—is

23

coined when the original word has lost its specificity. For example, after the invention of the digital watch, it was necessary to describe the old-fashioned, big-hand/little-hand timepiece as an "analog" watch. Urban (from the Latin *urbs*, meaning city, which itself is taken from Ur, believed to be the first city) ministry was for many years virtually the only ministry the church had. In the fifties, the church dutifully followed many of her members as they abandoned city churches and sought to live out the American dream in the suburbs, where newer, sleeker houses of worship were erected. Nowadays, urban ministry is really a code word for any of the church's work that happens to occur in the inner city. "Inner city" is, of course, a code word for neighborhoods inhabited by so-called minority groups, communities that often lack the financial base necessary to maintain the drafty Victorian Gothic edifices bequeathed to them by white flight to the suburbs, much less to sponsor and administer programs.

But urban ministry, far from being the invention of avant-garde theologians of the sixties, is as old as the Bible itself. It was from the city of Ur that Abraham responded to God's call to "let goods and kindred go" and to find the land that God would show him. It was the city of Nineveh, whose wickedness, like many a modern metropolis, "stares God in his face," that Jonah was called to denounce. It was the city of Babylon, and not some sylvan retreat, that served as the "strange land" where God's chosen people managed, despite their oppression, to sing the Lord's song. It was in the city of Bethlehem (which in Hebrew means "House of Bread"), during his parents' visit to pay taxes, that our Savior Jesus Christ, who was himself to become the Bread of Life, drew his first breath. The Apostle Paul preached the Gospel to the powerful and influential city of Rome—long before Constantine made Christianity respectable—and he battled against the beasts in the prosperous city of Ephesus. In Corinth, a city racked with immorality and licentiousness, Paul preached a gospel of love and forbearance.

In his book, *The City in History: Its Origins, its Transformations, and its Prospects*, Lewis Mumford wrote that "the medieval city in Europe may be described as a collective structure whose main purpose was the living of a Christian life. . . . At no point," he writes, "were medieval municipal institutions such as the hospital and alms house separated from the church, and at no point was the church separated from the community." It may well be, in this time of downsizings and retrenchments, that this medieval model will be a paradigm for urban life in this new millennium. It falls to all of us to make our urban centers earthly visions of the city of God, the heavenly Jerusalem.

Early in the twentieth century, Walter Russell Bowie, rector of Grace Church, New York City, laid out for us the challenge of urban ministry:

> O shame to us who rest content
>> while lust and greed for gain
> in street and shop and tenement
>> wring gold from human pain,
> and biter lips in blind despair
>> cry, "Christ hath died in vain!"
>
> Give us, O God the strength to build
>> the city that hath stood
> too long a dream, whose laws are love,
>> whose ways are brotherhood,
> and where the sun that shineth is
>> God's grace for human good.
>
> Already in the mind of God
>> that city riseth fair:
> lo, how its splendor challenges
>> the souls that greatly dare—
> yea, bids us seize the whole of life
>> And build its glory there.

James Russell Bowie, "O holy city, seen of John," *The Hymnal 1982*, No. 582

. . . . . .

IN THE SUMMER OF 1970, I found myself with Claudette, my bride of five months, in the family room of the *casa del obispo* in Guatemala City. We were engaged in a rather serious game of bridge with Bill Frey, the Bishop of Guatemala, and his wife Barbara. We had just completed an intense course in conversational Spanish in Cuernavaca, Mexico, and were on our way to put our learning to use in one of the missions on Guatemala's north coast. As it turned out, Claudette and I were assigned to the aptly named fruit company town of Bananera, where we lived with a fellow seminarian, Silvestre Romero (who years later would become Bishop of Belize). I don't remember who won the game with the Freys, but I do remember that a great friendship was forged as we were bidding three no-trump and quaffing the local *cerveza*.

I could not have imagined that, almost exactly a year later, the bishop would send a cable to me, a newly-minted deacon, to ask me to serve in Honduras, of which he was bishop-in-charge. A month after the cable arrived, Claudette and I boarded a banana boat in Staten Island, bound for Tela, Honduras. From Tela, we wended our way to La Ceiba, a hundred kilometers away, where I became priest-in-charge of a congregation, Iglesia Santísima Trinidad, and chaplain to its day school. But we made a weekly visit back to Tela, where, I discovered upon arrival, I would also be privileged to serve the people of another congregation, Iglesia Santo Espíritu.

Soon after settling at the rectory, we learned that Bishop Frey was to be expelled from Guatemala. He had spoken out rather forcefully against the totalitarian regime there, and he and his entire family were placed under house arrest and given seventy-two hours to quit the country. When Bishop Frey came to La Ceiba to ordain me to the priesthood three months later, the service became, as a result, a center of international intrigue. Since the bishop, who was living in exile in Fayetteville, Arkansas, could not reenter Guatemala, his clergy from there came to the ordination in La Ceiba and managed to have a clergy conference with their exiled father-in-God. Bill Frey's ordeal doubtless had an unwitting effect on my ministry. His example was one of a person willing to stand up and be counted, to suffer for Christ's sake. His witness brought to mind the stories I had heard of Bishop Manning of New York, who some forty years before, marched down Amsterdam Avenue, and with the help of the New York City Police and Fire Departments, broke the padlock on the door of All Souls' Church, whose wardens had decided to close the church instead of allowing the parish to integrate.

Christian leaders must decide whether they are going to be like Amos or like Amaziah. Amaziah was a court chaplain and sycophant. He saw it as his job to preach comfortable words to those ensconced in comfortable pews. He was hardly a boat rocker. He was the defender of civil religion. Amos, on the other hand—"a herdsman and a dresser of sycamore trees"—whom the Lord called to prophesy, spoke for the people. He was a champion of civil rights. The Lord had called him to denounce those who perpetrated injustices against the people of God. And so, like Amos, effective Christian leaders must be willing to take a plumb line to true the church, that is, to test its spiritual soundness, its doctrinal perpendicularity.

> Lord, you give the great commission:
>   "Heal the sick and preach the word."
> Lest the Church neglect its mission,
>   and the Gospel go unheard,
> help us witness to your purpose with renewed integrity;
>   with the Spirit's gifts empower us
>   for the work of ministry.

Jeffery Rowthorn, "Lord, you give the great commission," *The Hymnal 1982*, No. 528

. . . . . .

"Master of eager youth, controlling, guiding"

—The Hymnal 1940, No. 362

EXACTLY EIGHT DAYS after my ordination as a deacon, I was the preacher at a Youth Sunday celebration at St. George's Church, Brooklyn, a neighboring parish to St. Philip's, where I had grown up. My best friend's sister, who was active in the parish youth group, had asked the rector, Father Hucles (later Bishop Suffragan of Long Island), if I could be the speaker that day. She felt that I might be a good role model for the young people of the parish.

I was twenty-four years old; and I sported the requisite Afro of the period. I wore my brand new, tailored Wippell's cassock, and a pristine Wippell's surplice of almost equal length. Over my left shoulder was a green silk stole designed by the Holy Rood Guild. But, wait, there's more! My outfit was made complete by a pair of Jesus-like leather sandals, between the straps of which could be seen my exposed feet! I had done it, admittedly, for effect. I knew the congregation would be buzzing, and I was right. I can remember hearing, as I processed down the aisle, the muffled comments and whispers, and I can remember seeing the odd index finger pointing toward my pedal extremities. St. George's parishioners were largely tradition-bound West Indian Anglicans (in the early seventies, hats and gloves were still *de rigueur* for the ladies in the congregation). But here I was: at my first preaching engagement as a clergyman—someone who as an acolyte would not be allowed to serve at the altar without polished black shoes—with my toes exposed to the common gaze! I took my text from Jeremiah, emphasizing that the Lord did not accept the prophet's youth as a disqualification for service. I guess the people had gotten over the shock of my feet long enough to glean something from my homiletic offering. Ah, the rebellion, the brashness, and the folly of youth!

The incident is emblematic, perhaps, of the boyishness that—a stiff collar notwithstanding—clergy of my generation had not forsaken entirely. But in addition to our immaturity, we were also foolhardy enough to believe that we could save the world and revolutionize the church. Salt would be put on our tails soon enough. We would receive a whole bunch of reality checks. We would be upbraided, chastened. But for now, we who had participated in sit-ins to protest injustices and atrocities at home, and antiwar rallies to protest injustices and atrocities abroad, were full of zeal for the Gospel. "For Zion's sake, we would not keep our peace."

Not long ago, when bishops were faced with a drastic increase in those offering themselves for the sacred ministry, they made among themselves a kind of gentlemen's agreement not to accept young candidates. Thirty was almost universally seen as the lower limit for those who wished to *begin* the ordination process. This was an egregious error on the part of the church, compounded by the fact that most of the church's college chaplaincies, which had been a spawning ground for vocations, had been eliminated (maybe because those chaplains were encouraging their students to protest injustices and atrocities at home and abroad?). Bishops told those aspiring to ordination that they should get experience in the world, and then come back. Most of them didn't. Discouraged that the church did not value their youthful enthusiasm, they stayed at IBM, where their talents were appreciated and immediately put to use. The church, having come to grips with its myopia, now understands that the "glut" of clergy was made up of those "of riper years," who have since retired. The glut of twenty years ago is now a shortage. So throughout the church, bishops are frantically trying to replenish the ranks, with programs such as the Young Priests Initiative.

It is my prayer that the church will never again discourage young women and men who have a clear sense of call, and who—in the words of the old Ordinal—wish to "dedicate themselves wholly to this one thing." Let them come in, make a few mistakes, get some on-the-job training and become seasoned, dedicated priests with a zeal for the Gospel. And if

· · · · · ·

the church's gatekeepers are ever again tempted to discourage young vocations, they should read the advice that the Lord gave to Jeremiah: "Do not say 'I am only a youth.' For to all to whom I send you, you shall go, and whatever I command you, you shall speak. Be not afraid of them. . . . Behold I have put my words in your mouth" (Jeremiah 1:7–9).

> *Master of eager youth,*
> *   Controlling, guiding,*
> *Lifting our hearts to truth,*
> *   New power providing;*
> *Shepherd of innocence,*
> *Thou art our Confidence;*
> *To thee, our sure Defence,*
> *We bring our praises.*

F. Bland Tucker, "Master of eager youth," *The Hymnal 1940*, No. 362

. . . . . .

"Knitting severed friendships up"

—The Hymnal 1940, No. 590

LA CEIBA, HONDURAS, where I began my ordained ministry, was a fruit company town. Its entire infrastructure had been created by and maintained for the convenience of the fruit company. The fruit company, for instance, was the de facto telephone company, which meant that they decided who would have a telephone and who would not. Company *jefes,* mostly *gringos,* and a smattering of other highly placed people, had telephones. The rectory of the local Roman Catholic parish had a telephone, but la Iglesia Episcopal Santísima Trinidad was not high enough up on the totem pole to rate such a perk. Nowadays, I have seven lines at the church, two at home, faxes and E-mail in each place, not to mention the ubiquitous God forbid-I should-be-unreachable-for-a-minute cell phone; I find it hard to believe that I lived a year without benefit of even a party line phone at either home or office.

But life moved apace, nevertheless, and we didn't seem to suffer from problems due to lack of communication technology. Important messages were brought to the priest at the rectory gate. People dispatched their children or their yardboys with verbal or written communications. It was in such a manner that we normally learned of parishioners' deaths. Now there was no embalming there in those days, which meant that burial normally took place within twenty-four hours of death. A made-to-order coffin (not a polished oak and brass casket) was fabricated by the local carpenter; the body, bathed and shrouded, was placed in it, and "visitation" took place at home. Pallbearers carried the body from home to the church, where burial office was read and Requiem Mass was celebrated. An odds-on favorite funeral hymn was "Ten thousand times ten thousand," which for some inexplicable reason did not survive hymnal revision. It made such an impression on me that I have directed that it be sung at my own Requiem Mass. The words offer great comfort:

> O then what raptured greetings
> > On Canaan's happy shore!
> What knitting severed friendships up,
> > Where partings are no more!
> Then eyes with joy shall sparkle
> > That brimmed with tears of late;
> Orphans no longer fatherless,
> > Nor widows desolate.

Henry Alford, "Ten thousand times ten thousand," *The Hymnal 1940*, No. 590

The service concluded, the priest, on foot and in vestments, would lead the coffin through the streets of the town to the cemetery a mile and a half away. Opposing traffic stopped as the procession passed. At graveside, a lump of earth (rather than sand from a silver vial) was used to trace the cross on the coffin, and—while grave diggers covered the hole into which they had lowered the coffin without benefit of hydraulic equipment—the faithful sang hymns. It was in those days that I got into the habit of kissing the coffin. It seemed altogether fitting and proper, since I also kissed babies' foreheads after tracing the sign of the cross on them at Baptism.

The Central American experience helped to remind me of the basic dignity and simplicity of Anglican funerals. Funerals and Evensong are what Anglicans do best, and there have been not a few people so impressed by the burial office in an Episcopal Church that they returned out of curiosity to see how Episcopalians treat the living. Unfortunately, one of the myths that has been allowed to circulate in some Episcopal circles is that eulogizing is a no-no. The officiant at a funeral is, according to this "rule," only to preach on the Resurrection, in order to give hope to the bereaved. "Don't focus on the deceased," says the rule. Nonsense! An officiant who says absolutely nothing about the person in the casket comes across as aloof and indifferent, not characteristics that endear the reverend clergy to their people. In the spirit of Anglicanism, it is not either/or but both/and.

· · · · · ·

Once, admittedly, I pushed the envelope. A particularly colorful man died a few months after I arrived at Calvary, Pittsburgh. He was a witty, clever octogenarian with a host of nieces and nephews. He had been a llama farmer and limerick-writer. That was my clue. I preached at his funeral and ended the sermon like this:

> Poet Paul was a bright man with a keen intellect, who never ceased to delight those around him. And because he was especially fond of limericks, the preacher begs the indulgence of his family and friends, and asks to be exonerated of all charges of irreverence for offering the following in Paul's memory:

> There once was a man named Paul Scheetz,
> Accomplisher of many great feats;
> He approached Miss Rust's father,
> And said, "Sir, I'd rather
> Be Alice's, for my heart bleats."

> Journalist, poet, and farmer,
> Seldom irate but much calmer;
> Avuncular, witty,
> Displaying great pity
> For every niece, nephew, and llama.

> And so Paul, we bid you farewell,
> For if we the truth were to tell,
> We give God the glory
> For the wonderful story
> Your life's been, O servant, done well!

· · · · · ·

"A new creation comes to life and grows"

—*The Hymnal 1982*, No. 296

"IT MUST HAVE BEEN the trumpet stops, Mrs. Lewis."

With such pithy English wit did the chaplain of St. John's College, Cambridge, greet Claudette in the maternity ward of Mill Road Hospital. He was one of the procession of greater and lesser prelates and assorted academics who made pastoral calls on the new mother, much to the astonishment of her "townie" ward mates. The reference was to the fact that on the Sunday next before Advent, the night before going into labor, Claudette attended the service of Lessons and Carols in St. John's Chapel. With great difficulty she waddled down the aisle, sat on the pillow that I had placed for her on the pew, and listened to the choristers as they made a joyful noise unto the Lord. The next morning, we took the ambulance to the hospital, where eighteen hours later, Justin Craig Lewis came into the world. The breathing exercises we learned in Lamaze class proved to be less than helpful, since it was determined that a Caesarean would be necessary; and accordingly, Dr. Bright was roused from his slumber at 2 A.M., and Claudette was whisked away to meet him in the operating theater. An hour later, the nurse presented Justin to his groggy father, announcing, "Mr. Lewis, you have a son."

Justin was named for the first-century apologist and martyr and for Enid Beatrice Craig John, who came to England to witness the birth of her first great-grandchild. Thanks to "Gran Gran," a proper English pram was procured, a nurse was hired, and a nappy service was engaged, since new-fangled Pampers were deemed unsuitable! Enid John, a statuesque woman of almost regal bearing, was accustomed to having her way in all things. Twelve hours after Justin's birth, she arrived at the hospital and was told that the baby was in intensive care and could be visited only by his father. Mrs. John, raising an arm adorned with at least half a dozen gold bangles from her native St. Vincent, informed the hapless ward clerk that she had come all the way from New York to see her first great-grandchild, and had no intention of leaving without accomplishing her mission. She was admitted to ICU without any further delay.

The birth of a child, to borrow a phrase from the collect for All Saints' Day, is an "ineffable joy." It's partly an ego thing; it's partly an immortality thing; but mostly it's the realization that you have come as close as you ever will to being a partner with God in creation. To behold a new creature, equipped with your genes, for whom you will be responsible for providing physical, spiritual, and emotional nurture, is awesome. On 28 November 1972, bleary-eyed and ecstatic, I could not foresee that Justin, as a graduation speaker at St. Paul's School, would one day cause tears to well in his parents' eyes by declaring that his greatest support system at St. Paul's was that which was provided by his mom and dad. I could not yet envision the sense of pride we would feel as we cheered Justin on when he was rowing a boat or kicking a ball. We could not imagine the joy we would experience, sitting in a hushed auditorium as he flawlessly executed a Chopin prelude.

On the First Sunday after Epiphany, 1973, the Dean of Jesus College, Edward Rochie Hardy (who had once been my professor of liturgics at Berkeley Divinity School), mounted the steps to the font at Little St. Mary's, Cambridge, and baptized the said Justin Craig Lewis (who was wearing the same baptismal gown I had worn twenty-six years earlier), making him a child of God and an inheritor of the kingdom of heaven. Following the ceremony, we repaired to our flat in Lady Margaret Road, where the assembled well-wishers celebrated Justin's Baptism with the usual bubbly, and by eating a layer of our wedding cake. A traditional West Indian fruitcake, it had been soaked in Mount Gay rum every several weeks since our wedding, so as to preserve it for this very occasion.

A new creation comes to life and grows
as Christ's new body takes on flesh and blood.
The universe restored and whole will sing: Alleluia!

John Brownlaw Geyer, "We know that Christ is raised and dies no more" *The Hymnal 1982*, No. 296

. . . . . .

"Man with God is on the throne"

—The Hymnal 1982, No. 215

RULES OF ACADEMIC HABERDASHERY were strictly observed in St. John's College Chapel in the University of Cambridge. At Evensong on ordinary weekdays, members of college were expected to wear academic gowns over their street clothes. On feasts and their eves—and therefore on Sundays and Saturday nights—surplices were to be worn in lieu of gowns. Simple, lightweight surplices were supplied for this purpose, and could be collected from a hook in the narthex en route to one's stall. I noticed that, on such festive occasions, members of college also wore academic hoods over their surplices. Since I had brought with me my McGill hood, which, trimmed in *faux* ermine, looked very like the Cantabrigian variety, I fell into the habit of throwing it over my surplice on the appropriate occasions. Throughout the Michaelmas term, as we celebrated the virtues of such worthies as St. Luke the Evangelist and St. Andrew the Apostle, and the Lent term, when we gave Mary her due on the feasts of the Purification and the Annunciation, I turned up hooded.

Came the Feast of the Ascension of our Lord Jesus Christ. The Easter term had almost run its course. This was "an high day in Zion" at St. John's. Evensong was broadcast over the waves of the BBC. Music aficionados made it a habit to go to both King's College and St. John's to compare their respective choirs' renditions of the Ralph Vaughan Williams setting of Psalm 47, "God is gone up with a shout." Of course, I was ignorant of these traditions and their effect on chapel attendance, and was therefore surprised when, arriving two minutes before the beginning of the service, I was confronted with an overflowing congregation and a sign in the narthex that read, "Dead Silence." I quickly determined that wending my way conspicuously down the long, marble aisle was not an option, so I slipped into the

. . . . .

nearest stall I could find, which, as fate would have it, was adjacent to that of the President of the College. Dr. Cook shot me an "if-looks-could-kill" glance, and extended his thumb and forefinger, with which he inspected the satin, faille, and "ermine" of my hood as if preparing to purchase it. Then he uttered three, clipped, British monosyllables which have remained seared in my memory ever since: "What *is* that?" "B.A., McGill," I muttered, with as much dignity as I could muster. Then the President wagged in my face the same index finger he had used to examine my hood, and declared, "Not here, not here." At that moment the organ sounded, and as we rose, the verger appeared, dutifully followed by the choir boys clasping mortarboards to their chests.

I was later to discover that non-Cambridge hoods are never to be worn in Cambridge chapels. Even if a D.Phil. from Oxford is called to be a professor at Cambridge, a Cambridge degree is conferred upon that individual in order that he or she might appear in chapel properly hooded. Later still, I could meditate on the theological significance of *when* my Cambridge comeuppance took place. The Feast of the Ascension is the complement to the Divine Condescension that we celebrate in the Incarnation. Having completed his earthly work, Jesus returns to the right-hand of the Father, an event theologians call the Divine Session. But this event does not mark a separation from Jesus. Rather, it signals the inauguration of a new status for those of us "who confess and call ourselves Christians." We share in Jesus' Ascension in a very special way. It can be argued that it is at the Ascension that we, as believers, truly become *active* members of the Body of Christ, the Church. Unlike those men of Galilee, rebuked by the angel for "standing gazing into heaven" (Acts 1:11), we fully understand that it is our responsibility to *be* the living members of the body of Christ, to be his hands and feet; "to do the work he has given us to do, to love and serve him as faithful witnesses." The hymnwriter put it this way:

. . . . . .

Thou hast raised our human nature
    on the clouds to God's right hand;
there we sit in heavenly places,
    there with thee in glory stand.

Jesus reigns, adored by angels;
    Man with God is on the throne;
Mighty Lord, in thine ascension,
    we by faith behold our own.

Christopher Wordsworth, "See the Conqueror mounts in triumph," *The Hymnal 1982*, No. 215

This comes as no small comfort to one who suffered abject humiliation (a dose of which, my friends would agree, I sorely need from time to time) for the transgression of appearing in a Cambridge chapel with the wrong wedding garment, as it were. In "heavenly places," and in all those places where we move and breathe and have our being as we usher in the kingdom of Christ, ecclesiastical and academic haberdashery—and all other outward and visible signs of rank or station that humankind has devised—count for naught. We need only bring "our selves, our souls and bodies to be a reasonable, holy and living sacrifice." We needn't worry that the One who invites us with the words, "Come O blessed of my Father, inherit the kingdom prepared for you from the foundation of the world" (Matthew 25:34), will ever distance us with the words "not here, not here." I am ever indebted to Dr. Cook for helping me to put all this in perspective.

. . . . .

> *"Above the noise of selfish strife, we hear thy voice, O Son of man"*
> —The Hymnal 1982, No. 609

IN THE LATE NINETEENTH CENTURY, the Lower East Side was New York's melting pot, the next step after Ellis Island for many Eastern European immigrants. A century later, the immigrant pool was enlarged to include Asian Americans, Jews, and West Indians. It was in this neighborhood that the Episcopal Church struck a blow for the working classes in the twenties and thirties, fighting for decent housing and respectable pay scales. These initiatives may appear to be a tame form of outreach today, but—at a time when union demands for salary increases were considered immoral attempts to alter just compensation levels set by moral law—such advocacy was nothing short of revolutionary. In those days, little-remembered Episcopal organizations such as the Society of Christian Socialists, the Christian Social Union, and the Church Association for the Advancement of Labor were working hard to redress the injustice of widespread economic disparity. Anglo-Catholic parishes such as St. Augustine's on Henry Street (down the block from the famous Henry Street Settlement House) were often at the forefront of such activity.

I spent the summer of 1973 working at St. Augustine's. Ira Johnson, then a student from General Seminary, also was there that summer, and together we worked especially closely with the youth of the parish. We dealt with the hard challenges of urban life that these kids faced, and even now Father Johnson and I weep when we recall the three-week period in which we buried two young men from the group, both of whom had been victims of violence. But we remember the fun as well—the dances, the parties, the trips, the into-the-night discussions about everything under the sun. After I arrived at the parish, I learned the true meaning of "all other duties as assigned." The Hispanic vicar underwent surgery and was out for a month, so—rusty Spanish and all—I managed to do *la Misa en español* (with admittedly short sermons). The highlight of the week was the Sunday Eucharist. It was "High Church with soul." Kente cloth vestments, Gospel choir, and much incense. Arthur Mussenden, now a priest, was at that time the formidable master of ceremonies. If he pointed to something in the missal, you said it, or more than likely, intoned it. A gentle nudge at the elbow or a sideways glance meant "Genuflect now!" I made the mistake once (and only once) of questioning his liturgical judgment. He instructed me that, at the end of the service, I should sing the blessing. "I thought only bishops sang the blessing," I protested. "At St. Augustine's, everybody is a bishop," came the retort. I took a deep breath and did as I was told.

> *Where cross the crowded ways of life,*
> *where sound the cries of race and clan,*
> *above the noise of selfish strife,*
> *we hear thy voice, O Son of man.*
>
> *In haunts of wretchedness and need,*
> *on shadowed thresholds dark with fears,*
> *from paths where hide the lures of greed,*
> *we catch the vision of thy tears.*
>
> *O Master, from the mountain side,*
> *make haste to heal these hearts of pain;*
> *among these restless throngs abide,*
> *O tread the city's streets again.*

Frank Mason North, "Where cross the crowded ways of life," *The Hymnal 1982*, No. 609

"Our pride is dust, our vaunt is stilled, we wait thy revelation"

—The Hymnal 1982, No. 598

"CORPORATE COMMUNIONS" are standard fare in the liturgical diet of many of our parishes. On a given Sunday, the members of a guild or parish organization sit together in the front pews of the church and, at the time of communion, kneel at the altar rail and receive communion "as a body," ahead of other parishioners. I encountered the practice when, at the age of twenty-six and a priest for two whole years, I assumed the pastoral cure of St. Monica's, Washington, D.C. The custom of corporate communions struck me as elitist, even for Episcopalians. The singling out of a particular group within the parish, the special treatment they received, the public "strutting their stuff" all offended my sensibilities. It seemed unjustifiable, for pastoral as well as theological reasons. So one fine morning, during the announcements, I declared, by rectorial fiat, that the practice would be abandoned, effective immediately. Then I went on to talk about bake sales, committee meetings, and other events in the life of the parish.

The following Sunday, a group of ladies asked to see me immediately following the Eucharist. The delegation was headed by Mrs. Ernest P. Norwood, a septuagenarian who was a lifelong member of St. Monica's. She was treasurer emerita and had held various positions in the parish and the diocesan Episcopal Church Women, but it was clear from the identities of the other ladies in the delegation that Hilda Norwood was coming to me in her official capacity as president of the Daughters of the King. Even behatted and in heels, Mrs. Norwood, standing before the chancel steps, could not have been more than 5'5". But because of her elegant and commanding presence, she seemed to tower over my 6'2" frame. She got right to the point. "Father Lewis," she began, "we would like you to rescind your decision to discontinue corporate communions. The Daughters of the King have been having corporate communion at St. Monica's every third Sunday since 1942, *before you were born*. We don't do it because we think we are more important than other people, as you would suggest; we do it because it helps us prepare spiritually for our monthly meeting." Now I knew before she presented her case that Mrs. Norwood would prevail, so, even as she was speaking, I was formulating in my mind the most dignified way to accede to her request and yet maintain my authority. "Mrs. Norwood," I responded, "clearly it means a lot more to you to have corporate communions than for me *not* to have them, so I will rescind my decision." As she put on her gloves, she delivered the *coup de grace*. "Thank you, Father. It takes a big man to admit when he is wrong." And with that, she nodded to the other officers of the Daughters of the King, and corporately, they took their leave.

The lessons I learned from this encounter early in my ministry are legion. I learned that I should not, as St. Paul warned the Romans, "think of myself more highly than I ought to think." I learned that, as my good friend and colleague, Alonzo Pruitt (currently rector of St. Philip's, Brooklyn), reminds me, "Every hill is not a Golgotha." Otherwise put (if I may mix topographical metaphors), you have to choose which ditches you are willing to die in. I also learned something about "mutual ministry"—that decisions, especially, perhaps, those having to do with worship, are best made after consultation with the people who will be affected by the decision. But most of all, I learned that it's all right to make mistakes, as long as you're big enough to admit that you were wrong.

> *O wounded hands of Jesus, build in us thy new creation;*
> *our pride is dust, our vaunt is stilled, we wait thy revelation:*
> *O love that triumphs over loss,*
> *we bring our hearts before thy cross, to finish thy salvation.*
>
> Walter Russell Bowie, "Lord Christ, when first thou cam'st to earth," *The Hymnal 1982*, No. 598

· · · · · ·

"Often they were wounded in the deadly strife"

—The Hymnal 1982, No. 357

IT WAS DECEMBER 21, 1976. I remember the exact day because it was the fifth anniversary of my ordination to the priesthood. The phone was ringing when I came through the door of our house on Capitol Hill in Washington. It was my mother calling from Brooklyn. Freddy Martin, my oldest and closest friend, had been brutally murdered. I looked at my watch. It was about 3:00 P.M. I said a prayer for his soul. I called Claudette at her office to tell her what had happened, and I jumped in my car and drove to National Airport to catch the Eastern shuttle to LaGuardia. When I entered the home of Freddy's parents, I found a long queue stretching towards what had been Freddy's room before he moved into his own apartment. It was in his old room that his mother was receiving callers, having decided, apparently, that it was more appropriate to do it here, where Freddy's spirit was. When Mrs. Martin saw me, she rose. We embraced, and we cried—for what seemed like forever. Through the tears, vignettes of my friendship with Freddy flashed through my mind: summer day camp, petty mischief, boat rides, piano recitals, Sunday afternoon chess games, and, later, double-dating. We were only a month apart in age and lived a block away from each other, and for the dozen years or so that encompassed our childhood, prepubescence, adolescence, and young adulthood, we were inseparable. Freddy was the best man at our wedding, and I can still see his smiling, bearded face as he raised his glass and expressed the wish that we be blessed with "many *bambinos*." And now he was dead.

I flew back to Washington the next day. I'm not quite sure why, since I spent all of twenty-four hours there before returning to Brooklyn for the funeral. The Requiem Mass at St. George's was on the morning of Christmas Eve. The rector was kind enough to allow me to officiate at the graveside. This was the first time that I had ever performed these priestly acts for someone I had known so intimately. It was difficult, not just because of the emotions involved, but because it forced me to come to grips with my own mortality. But it was the least I could do for a friend whom I had loved so deeply.

Think, O Lord, in mercy
*   on the souls of those*
who, in faith gone from us,
*   now in death repose.*
Here mid stress and conflict
*   toils can never cease;*
there, the warfare ended,
*   bid them rest in peace.*

Often they were wounded
*   in the deadly strife;*
heal them, Good Physician,
*   with the balm of life.*
Every taint of evil,
*   frailty and decay,*
Good and gracious Savior,
*   cleanse and purge away.*

Edmund Stuart Palmer, "Jesus, Son of Mary," *The Hymnal 1982*, No. 357

. . . . . .

"Streams of mercy never ceasing, call for songs of loudest praise"
—Lift Every Voice and Sing II, No. 111

ON SATURDAY, MARCH 22, 1980, a torn and wrinkled airmail envelope arrived at my office at St. Monica's, Washington, D.C. The enclosed letter, dated in January, was penned by Bezaleri Ndahura, Bishop of Bukavu, Zaire, and the first archbishop of the new province of Burundi, Rwanda, and Zaire. The archbishop had appointed me his U.S. commissary, which meant that I represented his interests in the American church, including serving as a liaison between the province and companion dioceses as well as the World Mission department at our national church headquarters. In his letter, Archbishop Ndahura requested that I meet him in England on the Feast of the Annunciation, three days later, to serve as his chaplain at the enthronement of Robert A.K. Runcie as Archbishop of Canterbury. Archbishop Ndahura, with the twenty-seven or so other primates of the Anglican Communion, would be present to witness the installation of Dr. Runcie as the 101st successor to St. Augustine. After Evensong on Sunday, I found myself at Dulles airport, boarding a British Airways jet to Heathrow. I arrived in Canterbury in time for lunch on Monday, and tracked down Archbishop Ndahura.

I was greeted by good news and bad news. The good news was that I was to be appointed a canon of his diocese. "Ça donnera un peu de poids à l'office" (That will give a little weight to the office), he commented. The bad news was that, owing to space limitations, the primates of the Anglican Communion, for the first time ever, would not be attended by their chaplains at the enthronement. In other words, I was out of a job and, as it turned out, a seat! Attempts to remedy the situation—which included a petition laid at the feet of Presiding Bishop John Maury Allin—proved fruitless.

. . . . . .

The next morning, however, I put on my cassock, threw my surplice, tippet, and hood over my arm and walked down the hill from my hotel to the entrance of Canterbury Cathedral. I explained my plight to the policewoman at the gate, who apologized that she could be of no help, but suggested that I check with the Enthronement Office in the precincts. I slipped through the Alice-in-Wonderland-type archway and fought my way to it. An officious gentleman stood at his desk and cast a glance in my direction. Remembering Archbishop Ndahura's words, I announced: "I am Canon Harold Lewis, and I am Commissary and Senior Chaplain to His Grace, the Archbishop of Burundi, Rwanda, and Zaire." "What can we *do* for you, Canon?" enquired Mr. Officious. I explained my plight, and, at the end of my little speech, he took pity on me and said that he did have an obstructed view seat in one of the galleries. It was where bishops' wives were sitting. I accepted it and, an hour later, mounted the Dean's steps. When I arrived at the designated place, the view was obstructed less by pillars than by a sea of hats! But it was better than nothing, I said to myself, as I started toward an empty seat. At that very moment, a verger, wand in hand, appeared. Seeing me all dressed up and no place to go, as it were, he said, "Father, you have come in the wrong door." Without waiting for a response, he said, "Follow me." I dutifully followed him down winding medieval steps and emerged in a crypt chapel where the clergy of the Diocese of Canterbury were queuing up. As unobtrusively as I could, I went to the end of the line and, at the appointed hour, followed my brother clergy up another set of steps and into the apse of the Cathedral. But, as the clergy were instructed to fill in seats from the apse forward, I ended up in the very first row, not fifty feet from the throne of St. Augustine. Bishop Allin, who did a double-take as he entered the choir, said to me later at a reception, "Father, you lead a charmed life!"

This series of events is in many ways a parable of my life and ministry. I feel that both have been richly blessed. By the grace of God, doors have not only opened for me, they have been flung wide open. I have received, as the collect said, "more than I could have hoped for or desired." The Lord has allowed me to minister to all sorts and conditions of men and women "o'er every continent and island" of the Anglican Communion. When Bishop Hathaway of Pittsburgh interviewed me prior to my coming to Calvary, he asked if I had had any crises in my ministry. I responded that there had been professional ones, but never vocational ones.

The priesthood of Jesus Christ which it has been my privilege to share has been a joy. While the 1979 Prayer Book is an improvement in many ways, the incomparable words of the Ordinal in the 1928 Prayer Book still speak to me: "Have always therefore printed in your remembrance, how great a treasure is committed to your charge." It is a treasure of which we are unworthy stewards, and blessings come, and doors are opened, not by any merit of our own, but on account of God's grace that gives us power, "that God may accomplish his work which he hath begun" in us.

> *Come, Thou fount of every blessing,*
> *Tune my heart to sing thy grace;*
> *Streams of mercy never ceasing,*
> *Call for songs of loudest praise.*
> *Teach me some melodious sonnet,*
> *Sung by flaming tongues above.*
> *Praise the mount, O fix me on it,*
> *Mount of God's unchanging love.*

Robert Robinson, "Come, Thou fount of every blessing," *Lift Every Voice and Sing II*, No. 111

"Redeem the time; its hours too swiftly fly"

—The Hymnal 1982, No. 541

SEVERAL YEARS AGO, I was a candidate in an episcopal election, an essential part of which is the "dog-and-pony show." For the uninitiated, I should explain that the "dog-and-pony show" is the unofficial name for the series of interviews in which the candidates for bishop participate. In it, candidates (and their spouses) are expected to answer questions about their spiritual journeys, their leadership styles, and, of course, their views on the "burning issues."

As I prepared for the thirty-six appearances I would make during the six-day process in the diocese in question, I sought the counsel of a wise bishop. The advice of this wise bishop was sound, and although following it does not ensure election, I pass it on to anyone reading these words who aspires to the purple. The bishop said: "Harold, I know you think on your feet, and that the answer is forming on your lips before the question is fully phrased. But even though you think you know the answer, wait a few seconds; *look* like you're pondering the thought and *then* answer." Conventional wisdom is replete with recommendations that we take our time. "Haste makes waste"; "Marry in haste, repent at your leisure"; "Look before your leap." Emily Post used to (and perhaps still does) advise young ladies that it is unseemly to appear to be too eager to accept an offer of marriage, or even of a waltz, as it would make the ingenue look just a little too anxious, and detract from the desired impression on the suitor that she was a prize well worth the wait and uncertainty. "Patience," according to an old adage, "is a virtue."

Such conventional wisdom did not seem to prevail in first-century Palestine. Jesus, about the business of assembling the men who would come to be known as his disciples, walks by the Sea of Galilee (really a lake, of course) finds some burly, rugged fishermen about *their* business, and issues a simple invitation: "Follow me." And St. Matthew reports that "immediately they left their nets and followed him" (Matthew 4:26). Andrew and Peter left their boats, and James and John, who were helping their father mend his nets in order that they could go out for another catch, left Zebedee high and dry, presumably with a net full of holes. The disciples didn't ask where they were going, how long they would be gone, or even what they would be expected to do!

Even a cursory glance at the New Testament shows that everything of importance happens "immediately." The word (in the Greek, *eutheos*) occurs more than a hundred times. When Jesus was baptized in the River Jordan, he immediately rose from the water. The people whom Jesus healed were cured immediately. When Paul experienced his conversion, the scales fell from his eyes immediately. Even biblical animals get into the act. When Peter denied Jesus, "immediately the cock crowed."

Perhaps we need to reexamine conventional wisdom. Let's take a hard look at those things that cause us to act immediately. A sick child renders meaningless everything else in the universe. A response to an urgent plea from a friend in trouble is not postponed. A call from our trusted broker causes us to buy or sell without delay. Jesus conveys an urgency in building up the kingdom which we ignore at our peril. The opportunity to bring a neighbor to church and to Christ might not present itself again. The opportunity to evangelize by example may not knock twice.

> *Come labor on.*
> *Claim the high calling angels cannot share—*
> *to young and old the gospel gladness bear:*
> *redeem the time; its hours too swiftly fly.*
> *The night draws nigh.*

Jane Laurie Borthwick, "Come, labor on," *The Hymnal 1982*, No. 541

. . . . .

"Savior, like stars in thy right hand, let all thy Church's pastors be"

—*The Hymnal 1940*, No. 219

IT WAS THE FEAST OF ST. MATTHIAS, 1987. I sat in the chancel of St. John's Church on the island of St. Croix, resting my vocal chords after having just sung the litany at the consecration of E. Don Taylor as Bishop of the Virgin Islands. My eyes and ears were fixed on the pulpit on the opposite side of the chancel, where Bishop Richard Beamon Martin—formerly rector of the parish of my youth—was holding forth. I said to myself, "My goodness! He sounds just like me." A moment later, I realized that I had got it all wrong. It was I who, in my efforts to preach, had tried to sound like Bishop Martin. It was in that moment that I realized how much I had been affected by his weekly sermons delivered from the pulpit of St. Philip's, Brooklyn.

Bishop Martin is a clergyman of the old school. He gives new definition to "Christian gentleman." Always well-turned-out. Always gracious. But above all, he is a master of the homiletic art. When he preached at my institution as rector of Calvary, he mesmerized the congregation. He preached for forty minutes, *sans* notes, weaving stories in and out of his sermon without dropping a stitch. Whether preaching or engaging you in conversation in his living room, he made you realize that you are in the presence of a holy man. But his sanctity does not eclipse his pragmatism. He is a pastor. The advice he gave me, when early in my ministry I assumed duties at St. Monica's in Washington, D.C., stood me in good stead there and in subsequent cures: "You can make the parish machinery hum; you can double the budget, and erect new buildings; but unless you are there when your people need you, all else you do is for naught."

> *Within thy temple when they stand*
> *To teach the truth as taught by thee,*
>
> . . . . . .

Savior, like stars in thy right hand,
  Let all thy church's pastors be.

To watch, and pray, and never faint,
  By day and night strict guard to keep,
To warn the sinner, cheer the saint,
  To feed thy lambs, and fold thy sheep.

James Montgomery, "Lord, pour thy Spirit from on high," *The Hymnal 1940*, No. 219

. . . . . .

"Races and peoples, lo, we stand divided"

—The Hymnal 1940, No. 532

THERE WERE EIGHT OF US at the dinner table, half of the participants in a clergy leadership conference in which I was the sole nonwhite participant. We were engaging in the kind of clerical banter that is commonplace at such gatherings. We talked about how we were faring in our respective corners of the Vineyard—how many members we had in our congregations, the kind of outreach we were involved in, the status of building programs, and the size of budgets. Being on the national church staff at the time, and having no parish to brag about, I found myself involved in a sidebar with a bishop at the table. We reminisced and laughed about the "dog-and-pony show" in the diocese in which we had both been candidates, and which had culminated in his election. Our conversation was overheard by a retired priest across from us, who, out of the blue, looked at me and said "You must have felt like a mule in the Kentucky Derby. You couldn't have won, but at least you were in good company." The table was stunned into silence, and I remember to this day the image of forks frozen midair, as the processes of mastication and ingestion were suspended. Like me, my fellow diners could not believe what they had heard, but the tension that existed at that moment was due to a larger extent to their anticipation of what I might say in return. They were to be disappointed, however, for I decided to bridle my tongue. African Americans in this society, especially those of us who are male, over six feet tall, and weigh an eighth of a ton, develop a sixth sense. I knew intuitively that had I raised my voice and, even justifiably, "laced into" the septuagenarian priest, history would label me the culprit and him the victim, and the original provocation would long be forgotten. The nervous silence was broken by a "pass-the-salt" type comment and the meal was resumed.

I did have a private conversation with my colleague later, and, at first, this proved to be more painful than the incident. He honestly believed that he had said nothing wrong; suggested that his remarks were offered "as a joke," and that he really didn't think of me as black. He could not fathom any justification for my offense, and even opined that I was perhaps just a little too sensitive. But the two of us took Isaiah's advice: "Come, let us reason together though our sins be like scarlet." An hour and many tears later there was a mutual understanding that neither of us could have foreseen. Racism and sexism are often presented as twin evils in our society, and it is not my intention here to defend or refute that allegation. But suffice it to say that we are more adept at recognizing sexist behavior than we are at identifying racist behavior. Every American, prepubescent or older, knows what a sexist remark is, and often goes to pains to avoid making one, even if it means stifling a harmless compliment. But a wider berth is given when it comes to racist remarks, which the victim is often expected to "understand." Our nation's and our church's discomfort with the "R" word has led us in too many instances to pretend that racism does not exist. One of the more creative ways we have done this is to invent "multiculturalism," a laudable goal, but one we reach for with the well-intentioned superficiality of "I-sing-your-spiritual/you-eat-my-taco" Eighty years ago, the hymnwriter suggested that different races cannot begin to share their joys if they are unwilling to share their pains. Only meaningful, prayerful, and soul-searching dialogue leading to mutual understanding can begin to address what is still the number one social problem of our day, a problem that belies Christ's pure, unbounded love for all of us as children of God.

> Races and peoples, lo, we stand divided,
> And sharing not our griefs, no joy can share;
> By wars and tumults love is mocked, derided;
> His conquering cross no kingdom wills to bear:
> Thy kingdom come, O Lord, thy will be done.
> Laurence Housman, "Father eternal, ruler of creation," *The Hymnal 1940*, No. 532

"It is well with my soul"

—*Lift Every Voice and Sing II*, No. 188

ONE OF THE GREATEST JOYS I experienced while on the Presiding Bishop's staff was being a mentor to young men and women who were preparing for ordination. Ever since Father McFarlane tapped me on the shoulder nearly forty years ago, I have been intentional about returning the favor. At the end of their seminary course, many of these young people accorded me the privilege of preaching at their ordinations. One of these was Curtis Winfield Sisco, Jr., at whose ordination to the priesthood I preached in 1987. Curtis was a creative liturgist and a gifted musician. With these talents, he could whip together a liturgy for any occasion, be it Absalom Jones Day or Corpus Christi (the latter complete with canopy and rose petals)! I made sure that his gifts were put to use, and appointed him to the editorial committee of *Lift Every Voice and Sing II: An African American Hymnal,* for which he served as liturgical editor. Only Curtis could make the perfectly plausible argument that hymns like "Soon and very soon" and "We're marching to Zion" were appropriate for Advent. Curtis, a devoted parish priest, transformed St. Luke's, New Orleans, from a moribund, fractious community to a vibrant, altar-centered urban parish, loved and respected by the community for whom it had flung wide its doors, offering a wealth of outreach ministries.

Five and a half years after his ordination—with his ministry in New Orleans going great guns—Curtis was diagnosed with AIDS. When I asked him what I could do, he requested that I visit him once he returned to his home in Philadelphia in order that we could plan the funeral. About two weeks later, I hopped on the Metroliner, and dutifully presented myself at the home of Curtis's father. I sat at Curtis's bedside with a pen and a yellow legal pad, and assumed the role of *amanuensis,* as Curtis proceeded to dictate every detail of his funeral: every rubric, every collect, every lesson, every psalm, every hymn, every anthem;

· · · · · ·

which rite should be used; who the liturgical cast of characters should be. I had come with a Prayer Book and Hymnal, but they were not consulted. Curtis knew every page, every hymn number, even the name of the tune of each hymn. His final request was that I be the preacher and the Master of Ceremonies. So in November of 1992, I returned to the Church of St. Andrew and St. Monica in Philadelphia—where I had preached his ordination—to preach his funeral.

But Curtis had also given me strict instructions for the wake, to take place on the eve of the funeral. But it was to be preceded by a separate service that proved to be a deeply spiritual experience for all who participated. At this preliminary service, only the reverend clergy were present, and, as Curtis had dictated, we were to be clad in black cassocks. The body was brought in and placed (head first, the privilege of clergy) in the chancel, and was laid out in what Curtis had described as a priest's casket, whose entire lid could be removed. He was, like us, in a black cassock. While more than a score of priests sat in choir, reading appointed psalms, four of us had been given the responsibility of vesting our departed colleague—a final act of homage to our friend that gave new meaning to the words, "Thou art a priest forever." Clothing him with each vestment elicited for us the prayers we had learned to recite when vesting for Mass. We placed the amice, "the helmet of salvation," on his head, and then clothed him with an alb, symbolizing priestly purity. After the girdle, symbolizing spiritual watchfulness and a desire for temperance, was in place and properly knotted, we put on his stole, beseeching God that he might attain "everlasting felicity." Then came the maniple, placed over Curtis's left wrist. Rome had done away with it, and most Anglicans had followed suit, but Curtis always wore one, as a reminder that we did not abandon diaconal servanthood once "elevated" to the priesthood. Finally, we vested Curtis in his chasuble, the symbol of the joyful burden of the priesthood, and we recalled the words of the Prophet, "My yoke is easy and my burden is light." Then we placed a small chalice and paten in his hands. The vesting completed, and bier lights in place, the west doors of the church were opened and his family and friends entered the nave. As they filed by Curtis, soloists offered musical tributes. After the Litany at the Time of Death was sung, more music followed; the lid was placed on the casket and draped with a pall; then, according to Curtis' instructions, his biretta was placed on top of it, the bladeless side south (at his left ear). The following morning, at the Pontifical Requiem Mass, I ended my homiletic offering with these words:

> And now Jesus Christ, by the power of the Resurrection, has opened up for Curtis the gates of everlasting life. Curtis has been appointed chief sacristan and assistant organist in those heavenly precincts "where sorrow and pain are no more, neither sighing, but life everlasting." He has had to cut slits in his voluminous Wippell's surplice so that the feathers of his wings will not be ruffled; and he has suggested to the Almighty that the celestial choir, accustomed to singing Mozart's *Coronation Mass* and Bach's *Mass in B Minor*, might also sing Lena McLin's *Eucharist of the Soul*, at least occasionally. And so Curtis, content in that place "where no troubles distractions can bring" can now belt out:

> > *And, Lord, haste the day when the faith shall be sight,*
> > *The clouds be rolled back as a scroll,*
> > *The trump shall resound and the Lord shall descend,*
> > *Even so—it is well with my soul.*

And the heavenly choir, in chorus with angels and archangels, with prophets, apostles and martyrs, with the Blessed Virgin Mary, with blessed Luke, blessed Monica, blessed Absalom, and all the saints, shall take up the refrain:

> > *It is well—with my soul.*
> > *It is well, it is well, with my soul.*

> Horatio Spafford, "It is well with my soul," *Lift Every Voice and Sing II*, No. 188

. . . . . .

"Join hands, then, brothers, of the faith, whate'er your race may be"
—The Hymnal 1940, No. 263

THE SENIOR WARDEN explained that there would be a meeting with the vestry which was not in the original search-process schedule, because, "when it hits the papers in the morning," he wanted the members of the vestry to have met me, so that they could "defend their choice." "It" was my election as fifteenth rector of Calvary Church. And hit the papers it did. "White Church Calls Black Rector," read the title of the article, falling all too predictably into the pattern observed by the late Robert Hood, who wrote in *Social Teachings in the Episcopal Church* that "it is still newsworthy in the Episcopal Church when a black gets elected rector of a white parish."

The vestry and search committee were miffed. Calvary, first of all, was healthily integrated, hardly lily-white; and secondly, they resented the implication that the new rector was chosen because of his race. But they knew that this was the "man-bites-dog" angle that sells newspapers. And the search committee members were familiar with the comment in my book, *Yet With a Steady Beat*, that, in the history of the Episcopal Church, more blacks had been elected bishop than had been called to predominantly white congregations. All of us involved in the process knew of the legacy of race relations in the Episcopal Church, which, among other things, mandated clergy deployment along strict racial lines. Forty years ago, the vice president of the Episcopal Society for Cultural and Racial Unity (ESCRU) commented:

> The problem of racial relations is the number one social problem of our day. As such, it is the number one challenge before the Christian Church. . . . If, through God's grace, we rise to this challenge, future generations may look back on our day and declare, 'it was then that the Christian Church began to live the Faith it proclaims.'

. . . . .

There is a television commercial for Hebrew National hot dogs. An unseen, dulcet-toned announcer explains that other hot dog manufacturers put non-meat filler in their franks, but that Hebrew National is forbidden to do so because it observes Kosher standards. Then the camera pans to the sky, and the voice says: "Because we answer to a higher authority." As Christians we answer to a higher authority. Mindful of St. Paul's advice to the Romans that we not be "conformed to this world," we should not take our cue from the mores of society. We should rather "be transformed by the renewal of our minds, that we may prove what is the will of God, what is good and acceptable and perfect" (Romans 12:2). The church is at her best when she is seen "with the cross of Jesus going on before," and not, as is too often the case, with the cross of Jesus bringing up the rear! My decade at the national church headquarters taught me, among other things, that posters and programs dreamed up by the Presiding Bishop's staff and the proclamations, pronouncements, and promises of General Convention do little to effect changes in people's hearts. My experience at Calvary has taught me that there is no substitute for the experience of clergy and people living and working and learning from each other as children of God, as fellow pilgrims along the way. In this way we can hope to show that "there is neither Jew nor Greek, there is neither slave nor free, there is neither male nor female, for we are all one in Christ Jesus" (Galatians 3:28).

> *Join hands, then, brothers of the faith, whate'er your race may be!*
> *Who serves my Father as a son is surely kin to me.*
>
> *In Christ now meet both East and West, in him meet South and North,*
> *All Christly souls are one in him, throughout the whole wide earth.*
>
> John Oxenham, "In Christ there is no East or West," *The Hymnal 1940*, No. 263*

*The first tune of this hymn was arranged by Harry T. Burleigh, a renowned African American composer and arranger of spirituals. When in the 1890s he was chosen to be the baritone soloist in the choir of St. George's, New York City, many in the congregation objected, and threatened to withhold their pledges. A parishioner who supported Burleigh vowed to restore to the church's coffers every pledge so withdrawn. The church members' bluff was called, and Harry Burleigh sang in St. George's choir for fifty years. The parishioner's name was J.P. Morgan.

· · · · · ·

> *"All things wise and wonderful, the Lord God made them all"*
> —The Hymnal 1982, No. 405

WHEN CLAUDETTE AND I were on vacation in California a few years ago, we wended our way down Seventeen Mile Drive. We took in the sights during this romantic getaway—the breathtaking seaside golf courses, the dramatic coastline, and the multimillion-dollar estates of the rich and famous. After such hard work, we were a little hungry, and decided to check out the deli in Pebble Beach, where you can get a sandwich or an upscale picnic basket packed with pâté and Brie. We opted for the sandwich.

Across the road from the deli was a florist, and we stopped to smell the roses and the other flowers there. Claudette's eye was taken by several spectacular birds of paradise. But oddly, they seemed to be odorless. And just as we were beginning to think that our olfactory organs had failed us, the proprietor informed us, "These are permanent flowers." "Excuse me," I replied. And when she repeated herself, it dawned on me what she meant. These were what we poor, politically incorrect slobs call artificial flowers. I looked up at the sign on which was etched the name of the establishment: "Floresque," it read. Oh, I see, flower-*like*. I looked around me. All of the flowers here were "permanent."

"Permanent flowers" takes euphemism to a new level. I can deal with garbage men as sanitation engineers, and homemakers as domestic engineers. And if you insist that Fido and Tabby are no longer pets but animal companions, no problem. But permanent flowers? Seems sacrilegious. I was content with real flowers made by God and artificial flowers made by man. But now that artificial flowers are permanent, what does that make real, God-made flowers? Temporary? Terminal? In the phrase "permanent flowers" is summed up the heresy of the age: a notion that we mere mortals are calling the shots. What happened to the old notion that God is on the throne? Have we chucked the words of the psalmist: "It is he that

. . . . . .

has made us and not we ourselves?" Are we to become Christianesque, unable to sing, "We are the sheep of his pasture, and the sheep of his hands?"

As my eye (but not my nose) took in Floresque's inventory, the words of an old children's hymn served as a reality check:

> *Each little flower that opens,*
> *each little bird that sings,*
> *he made their glowing colors,*
> *he made their tiny wings.*
>
> *He gave us eyes to see them,*
> *and lips that we might tell*
> *how great is God Almighty,*
> *who has made all things well.*
>
>> *All things bright and beautiful,*
>> *all creatures great and small,*
>> *all things wise and wonderful,*
>> *the Lord God made them all.*

Cecil Frances Alexander, "All things bright and beautiful," *The Hymnal 1982*, No. 405

"Many a blow and biting sculpture polished well those stones elect"

—*The Hymnal 1982*, No. 519

CALVARY CHURCH, PITTSBURGH, is a magnificent example of turn-of-the-century Gothic Revival, a masterpiece of the renowned architect Ralph Adams Cram. The Cadet Chapel at West Point, as well as St. Thomas Church and the Cathedral of St. John the Divine in New York City, are also part of Cram's rich legacy, a legacy that present generations are privileged to preserve for posterity. As rector of Calvary, I am also *de facto* curator of an historic landmark, and, understandably, I have learned more in the past four years about stained glass, oak, and stone than I would have thought possible. In anticipation of a study soon to be undertaken which will examine the status of the church's mortar, our architect, Gerald Allen, wrote the following:

> Mortar is known as a sacrificial material, designed to wear away in the process of protecting a more valuable material. So not only does mortar close the joints between stones, it also provides a very slight degree of flexibility, so that as a building settles over time, or is subjected to the expansion and contraction caused by changes in temperature, the mortar absorbs these stresses which otherwise might crack the stones. For that reason mortar, when it has completed its sacrificial role, needs to be replaced on a routine basis. The perils of doing this . . . are legion. One of the worst is the careless use of electric saws or grinders to cut out the old mortar. These often cut out large areas of stone in the process, resulting in huge mortar joints where originally there were very thin ones. Another is the careless choice of mortar color, resulting in inappropriate matches with the stone and other mortars. Finally, in a misguided attempt to make the mortar more durable, it is sometimes formulated with so much

· · · · ·

Portland cement that it ends up harder than the adjacent stone and thus completely defeats its original purpose.

Although written about the preservation of a church building, Mr. Allen's words, at another level, are instructive to us to whom is entrusted the preservation of the church as the Body of Christ. St. Peter, after all, calls us "living stones built into a spiritual house, to be a holy priesthood, to offer spiritual sacrifices acceptable to God through Jesus Christ" (1 Peter 2:5). Our responsibility is to be, if you will, the mortar that helps keep the house of God together, a house built upon the foundation of Jesus Christ, the head cornerstone. As such, we are certainly sacrificial, as we offer our selves, our souls, and bodies only for as long as we have breath, from the time the cross is traced on our forehead in Baptism until the time it is traced, with earth, on our coffin. Other "mortared" Christians have preceded us, and many more will follow us. We must protect the church, but not stifle her. Since "new occasions teach new duties," we must give her room to adjust and adapt to the exigencies of time, so that she may speak to each age with integrity. We must be careful, lest, willy-nilly, we cut away that which is essential to the faith, necessitating our replacing it with doctrines of our own making, incompatible with the faith once delivered to the saints. As the mortar in Christ's house, the people of God must be strong enough to withstand the tempests that perennially assault the church, but be flexible enough to allow the wind of the Holy Spirit to infuse her.

Many a blow and biting sculpture polished well those stones elect,
in their places now compacted by the heavenly Architect,
who therewith hath willed for ever that his palace should be decked.

Latin, ca. 7th Century, John Mason Neale, trans. with other alterations,
"Blessèd city, heavenly Salem," *The Hymnal 1982*, No. 519

. . . . . .

"Endue the bishops of thy flock with wisdom and with grace"

—Hymns Ancient and Modern Revised, No. 472

BISHOP WALTER DECOSTER DENNIS was one of the many clergy whose prophetic witness served as an inspiration to me. At a service of Solemn Evensong in the Cathedral of St. John the Divine in New York City, at which the assembled congregation gave thanks for his four decades of service to the church, Bishop Dennis made some poignant comments. He observed that beginning in the mid-fifties, the church was becoming passionate on matters like integration and economic justice. He characterized the period roughly corresponding to the first half of his ministry, which was an era in the church of outward commitment to social concerns, as the "Age of Alphabet Soup and Acronyms": there was MRI (Mutual Responsibility and Interdependence); SRI (Social Responsibility in Investments); ESCRU (Episcopal Society for Cultural and Racial Unity); GCSP (General Convention Special Program); and SWEEP (Service, Worship, Evangelism, Education and Pastoral Care). Today, however—the bishop opined—the church has become inwardly focused: preoccupied with such matters as the authority and jurisdiction of bishops; the role of provinces in the Anglican Communion; and the relationship between bishops and clergy.

There have been many opinions voiced as to why the Episcopal Church has lost roughly a third of its membership in the period in question. Some say that it is due to a watering down of the doctrine, a diminishment of the discipline, and wanton experimentation with the worship of the church. Others have suggested that there has not really been a loss of people at all. Those who have left were only the "sprinklers" anyhow—those who came to church to be sprinkled with water at Baptism, rice at marriage, and dirt at death. While there is probably no one identifiable reason, clearly a significant factor has been the church's navel-gazing mode of existence, the inward focus of which Bishop Dennis spoke. Energy spent on such internal matters as Prayer Book revision, the ordination of women, and now the preoccupation with human sexuality has sapped the church of energy she would otherwise be using to usher in the kingdom.

Bishop Dennis went on to admonish that the role of all ministers—every bishop, priest, deacon, and layperson—is to enhance and enlarge the office to which he or she has been called, and not to diminish or lessen it. The Gospel mandate, he observed, is summed up in the sixty-first chapter of Isaiah, the text Jesus used for his first sermon: "The Spirit of the Lord God is upon me, because he has anointed me to preach good news to the poor . . . to proclaim release to the captives . . . to set at liberty those who are oppressed." This will be the Gospel, Walter Dennis declared, when all the church's fads and causes have run their course.

> *Endue the Bishops of Thy flock*
> *With wisdom and with grace,*
> *Against false doctrine, like a rock,*
> *To set the heart and face.*

> *To all Thy Priests Thy truth reveal,*
> *And make Thy judgments clear;*
> *Make Thou Thy Deacons full of zeal,*
> *And humble and sincere.*

John Mason Neale, "The earth, O Lord, is one wide field," *Hymns Ancient and Modern Revised*, No. 472

· · · · · ·

"Let each heart prepare a home"

—The Hymnal 1982, No. 76

I FOUND MYSELF IN NEW YORK one Wednesday early in December a few years ago, and decided to seek the refuge of St. Thomas Church, where I could attend a late afternoon celebration of the Holy Eucharist. As I headed north on Fifth Avenue, I discovered I could barely navigate the sidewalks. Shoppers and tourists were packed about eight or nine deep, and the police had even allowed them to spill over into the street. Surely these weren't just Christmas shopping crowds, I thought—and then it dawned on me: Wednesday was the day that the Rockefeller Center Christmas Tree would be lit! And people turned out by the thousands to witness this annual ritual, officially marking the beginning of "the Christmas season."

Meanwhile, back at the church, we're just a little out of step, insisting on squeezing the season of Advent, with its comparative doom and gloom, between Thanksgiving and Christmas revelings. In Matthew's Gospel we read about crowds gathering in great numbers, not to see thousands of bulbs lit up, but to see a rather eccentric, ill-clad, unkempt, and probably smelly character called John the Baptist. Some came out because they thought he was "the new Elijah." Others came because they wanted to be in on the ground floor, as the way was being prepared for the coming of the Savior. Still others came to heed his message of repentance.

Now "repentance" is not a word that easily flows from the lips of Episcopalians. And maybe that's our problem. There may well be a correlation between our unwillingness or inability to acknowledge the validity of repentance and the fact that we have lost a third of our members in the space of a generation. Perhaps we believe that the idea of repentance smacks of fundamentalism, and we associate it, therefore, with the fanatic on the corner (not

65

unlike John the Baptist) who carries a placard urging us to repent because the kingdom of God is at hand. If repentance seems alien to us, it's probably because sin is just as foreign a concept.

No, we don't take repentance very seriously. Indeed, we have perfected several evasive techniques that make it unnecessary for us to ever really repent. We avoid responsibility for what we have done wrong. Like the late comic Flip Wilson, we say "the devil made me do it." Or we blame it on society, or the church, or the times in which we live. Or we make the other guy the sinner. But all of our explaining it away notwithstanding, the idea of repentance is inextricably woven into our liturgy. It starts at Baptism. The priest asks the candidate: "Do you renounce the evil powers of this world which corrupt and destroy the creature of God?" And later asks: "Do you turn to Jesus Christ and accept him as your Savior?" And in the service of Morning Prayer, in some of the most beautiful words ever to flow from the pen of Thomas Cranmer, we express the meaning of repentance in prose both lofty and theologically unassailable:

> We have erred, and strayed from thy ways like lost sheep. We have followed too much the devices and desires of our own hearts. We have offended against thy holy laws. We have left undone those things which we ought to have done; And we have done those things which we ought not to have done; And there is no health in us. But thou, O Lord, have mercy upon us, miserable offenders. Spare thou those who are penitent.

If "repentance" is too churchy a word, let's try "turning around" or "change of heart," which, if I remember correctly, is the sense of the original Greek word, *metanoia*. Or, if we are more at home with the language of psychology or pop culture, how about "behavioral modification," "attitudinal adjustment," or "paradigm shift?" Whatever we call it, let's try it. Let's mend a fence, bury a hatchet, apologize. And if we try it, we will

. . . . . .

see that John the Baptist wasn't so crazy after all. His less than genteel barging into our pre-Christmas lives becomes not so much an intrusion as an opportunity, with the hope that Christmas might become, not a sentimental and perfunctory holiday, but a sacred and perfected holy day.

> *Then cleansed be every breast from sin,*
> *make straight the way of God within;*
> *and let each heart prepare a home*
> *where such a mighty guest may come.*
>
> Charles Coffin, "On Jordan's bank the Baptist's cry," *The Hymnal 1982*, No. 76

"O shepherds greet that glorious sight, our Lord a crib adorning"

—*The Hymnal 1982*, No. 91

CHRISTMAS HAS ALWAYS BEEN very special at our house, as we "bring out of our treasure what is new and what is old" (Matthew 13:52). Ornaments made by Justin in nursery school, others procured at our favorite vacation spots, are hung on the tree with appropriate historical and sentimental commentary. Another of our Christmas traditions is watching old holiday movies like *It's a Wonderful Life,* with Jimmy Stewart, or *The Bishop's Wife*, with Loretta Young in the title role, and the supercilious David Niven as her husband. But our award for the most theologically insightful Christmas movie goes to *Miracle on 34th Street.* When the young Natalie Wood asks her mother if she should believe in Santa Claus, Maureen O'Hara responds: "Faith is believing in things when common sense tells you not to."

Common sense is not what brings both regular and occasional worshipers to church at Christmas. Common sense tells us that "virgin birth" is an oxymoron. Common sense makes us wonder if there were really a maligned innkeeper, angels singing sweetly through the night, cattle lowing, and shepherds abiding in the field. We intuitively know what one theologian has said: that the details of the Christmas narrative "communicate the mystery of redemption, not a diary of early events." Yet we lustily sing Christmas carols containing all these references with great feeling and conviction. Why? Because at Christmas, more than at any other time, we realize that common sense just won't cut it! We come to church at Christmas because the whole experience is a sign of things that are greater than what we can perceive with our senses.

Christmas is a sign of calm in the midst of anxiety. We leave outside the bedlam of the season—the shopping, the wrapping, the overindulging, the scurrying back and forth. And we exchange all this for a moment at the crèche, where we sing "All is calm, all is bright." The world stands still as God takes on human form and becomes Emmanuel, God with us. Everything else—tree, lights, presents—pales before the crèche. *Christmas is a sign of stability in the midst of confusion.* Who can keep up? In a world in which the lines between veracity and mendacity are daily blurred, we welcome the opportunity to listen to the tidings of great joy, unequivocally proclaimed by the angel: "Unto you is born this day in the city of David a Savior which is Christ the Lord." *Christmas is a sign of peace in the midst of all the wars, large and small, that we human beings continue to wage.* As we struggle in vain to beat our swords into plowshares and our spears into pruning hooks, we are reminded that it was a message of peace that the angels sang to herald Jesus' coming into the world.

Maureen O'Hara was right. Common sense has its limitations. When we try to solve really important problems, when we grapple with issues of great consequence, when we attempt to find the meaning of life, we turn to our faith. Perhaps Miss O'Hara had this verse from the Epistle to the Hebrews in mind: "Now faith is the substance of things hoped for, the evidence of things not seen" (Hebrews 11:1).

> *Break forth, O beauteous heavenly light, and usher in the morning;*
> *O shepherds, greet that glorious sight, our Lord a crib adorning.*
> *This child, this little helpless boy, shall be our confidence and joy,*
> *The power of Satan breaking, our peace eternal making.*
>
> Johann Rist, "Break forth, O beauteous heavenly light," *The Hymnal 1982*, No. 91

· · · · ·

"The mount of vision: but below the paths of daily duty go"
—The Hymnal 1940, No. 571

WE HAVE ALL HAD MOUNTAINTOP experiences of one kind or another. Some are religious. The great mystics describe experiences in which they have, through intense prayer, meditation, or even suffering, entered into an intimate relationship with the Almighty. They see visions, they are enraptured, they feel the hand of God. Ours may be less dramatic but no less meaningful. Maybe it is a conversion experience, in which we make a conscious decision to accept Christ, or an uplifting experience of worship or prayer that in some way afforded us a glimpse of the heavenly Jerusalem here on earth. At times even a tragic experience—the loss of a loved one, or a protracted illness—can have the effect of bringing us closer to God. Martin Luther King, Jr. said that he had seen the mountaintop. Having experienced the closeness of God, having seen God's hand at work, having "walked with him and talked with him" during this earthly pilgrimage, he felt prepared to see his Lord face to face on the other side of Jordan. Of course, there are other types of mountaintop experiences, like being in love, or celebrating the attainment of some great milestone or life's goal.

The Transfiguration (Mark 9:2–9 and Luke 9:28–36) is the quintessential mountaintop experience. On the crest of Mount Tabor, Jesus is transfigured, his raiment becomes dazzling white. He has brought not the entire retinue of disciples, but his executive committee, Peter, James, and John. Moses and Elijah appear in glory, and the voice of God comes out of a cloud. It is a Cecil B. DeMille moment! Then the impetuous, foot-in-mouth Peter comes up with a brilliant idea—to build three tabernacles, one for Jesus, one for Moses, and one for Elijah. He wants to capture the moment and freeze it. In short, he wants his mountaintop experience to last forever. Jesus vetoes that idea, swears the disciples to secrecy, and descends from the mountain.

. . . . . .

But if we bother to read the verses that follow, we see that, immediately after this great mystical experience, Jesus is confronted with a distraught father whose only son is suffering from epileptic seizures. Jesus summons the child to him, rebukes the evil spirit, heals the child, and gives him back to his father. It is no accident that this story follows the Transfiguration. It reminds us that we must be sustained by our mountaintop experiences, see them as glimpses of glory, and use them to strengthen us to do the work that Jesus has given us to do. We who profess and call ourselves Christians must be willing to leave the tabernacles we so readily erect in order that we might cast out the demons of fear, injustice, and oppression that lurk just at the bottom of the hill.

> Not always on the mount may we
> Rapt in the heavenly vision be:
> The shores of thought and feeling know
> The Spirit's tidal ebb and flow.
>
> Yet hath one such exalted hour
> Upon the soul redeeming power,
> And in its strength, through after days,
> We travel our appointed ways.
>
> The mount of vision: but below
> The paths of daily duty go,
> And nobler life therein shall own
> The pattern on the mountain shown.

Frederick Lucian Hosmer, "Not always on the mount may we rapt in the heavenly vision be,"
The Hymnal 1940, No. 571

. . . . . .

"Just as I am, without one plea"

—The Hymnal 1982, No. 693

ONE OF THE PHRASES I remember from freshman Latin is *vestis virum facit* ("clothes make the man"). The Romans obviously believed that there were togas, and then there were togas. Things haven't changed much in the last two thousand years. Ever since the poor man in St. Matthew's Gospel came to the reception without a wedding garment and suffered dire consequences (Matthew 22:11–13), one of the most egregious of *faux pas* we can commit is to arrive at an affair either overdressed or underdressed. When I was in college, we had to wear jackets and ties for all our meals. When I came home on vacations, Claudette had to remind me more than once that I didn't have to dress so formally when I came a-courting.

All of us go through the daily ritual of deciding what to wear. We transform ourselves into the role we are playing that day—party animal, churchgoer, corporate executive. We decide not to look too flashy for a job interview, but on other occasions throw caution to the wind with a jaunty bow tie. Usually, our sartorial transformation is harmless, but sometimes it isn't. Jon Benet Ramsay was made into a tawdry beauty queen while still a toddler. Not infrequently, an inner-city youth dresses himself up like a Nike billboard only to discover that his fashion statement has attracted the kind of covetous attention that endangers his very life.

Just prior to Jesus' Crucifixion, the soldiers decide to dress Jesus up in a way befitting this so-called "King of the Jews." But or course, it is only the soldiers' cruel idea of a joke. They clothe him in a loose, reddish-purple outer garment, and pretend it is a robe of state. They take a thorny branch bent into a circle, and go through the motions of a coronation as they place it on Jesus' head. They put a rod in his right hand to make it look like a scepter. Then, after they mockingly bow before him, shouting "Hail, King of the Jews," they express their true feelings. They spit in his face and use the scepter-like staff to beat him about the head.

72

Jesus becomes a laughingstock. But when this little charade is over, they remove the clothes with which they mocked him and return the cloak he was wearing upon his arrival at the Praetorium. Normally a criminal condemned to crucifixion was paraded naked to his death, but Jesus is led off dressed *in his own clothes* (Matthew 27:31).

Some commentators believe that Jesus' own clothes were put back on him to spare him the indignity of being paraded naked through the streets of Jerusalem. But I would like to suggest another theory. Jesus wore his own clothes because it was in his own right that he went forth to suffer. He didn't go forth as the blasphemer, the heretic, or the traitor that his accusers said he was. He went forth neither as the king in whose path the people strewed palm branches, nor as the make-believe king of the bored soldiers. He went forth as the Son of God, the Incarnate Lord, the Savior of the world.

Ultimately, each of us must be accountable to our God —the God from whom no secrets are hid —in our own right. We will not have the luxury of donning different costumes to reflect the moods in which we find ourselves or the roles which others have assigned us. And I'm not just talking about Judgment Day. Almost daily we are faced with situations in which we must decide between being ourselves, standing for what we believe, or reaching for a convenient mask through which to speak. Jesus, in his own clothes, knew who he was and *Whose* he was. We pray that God will grant us the same gift of self-knowledge.

> *Just as I am, without one plea, but that thy blood was shed for me,*
> *and that thou bidd'st me come to thee, O Lamb of God, I come, I come.*
>
> *Just as I am, though tossed about, with many a conflict, many a doubt;*
> *fightings and fears within, without, O Lamb of God, I come, I come.*
>
> *Just as I am, thy love unknown has broken every barrier down;*
> *now to be thine, yea thine alone, O Lamb of God, I come, I come.*
>
> Charlotte Elliott, "Just as I am," *The Hymnal 1982*, No. 693

> *"God, the mighty maker, died for His own creature's sin"*
>
> —*Lift Every Voice and Sing II*, No. 30

"BLOOD IS THICKER THAN WATER," goes the saying that holds up familial relations as the strongest of the bonds human beings can have for one another. The bonds between members of the same family are strongest because, ostensibly, they will have the most in common. Shared ancestry means shared characteristics. The more similar people are, the stronger will be their bonds. The same principle radiates outward from the family and the extended family to cement the bonds of community.

"Community" is one of the most overused and, therefore, misused words in the double talk and journalese that pass for the Queen's English nowadays. In the gospel according to *The New York Times*, "community" is defined as any loosely-connected group of individuals who share some arbitrarily and externally determined characteristic. This sense of community is usually invoked to suggest to the reader that everyone in the group in question concurs on some particular point. The characteristic on which such a meaning of community is based may be racial, such as in the headline: "African American community supports Gore." It may refer to sexual orientation, as in "Gay community decries Clinton administration don't-ask-don't-tell policy." Or the characteristic may be ideological, as when we read to our horror: "Pro-life community condones violence at abortion clinics."

But I like to think that the quintessential community is the church. In the church, community begins, not with our similarities, but with our differences. In this community, water—the water of Baptism—is thicker than blood; the water of Baptism unites us, and transcends every conceivable difference we can imagine.

Now it is commonly held that the church came into existence at Pentecost, when the Holy Spirit descended upon the first Christians making it possible for the Parthians, Medes,

· · · · · ·

74

Elamites, and all those other ethnic groups to understand each other. But the Day of Pentecost, I believe, was really the birthday party, the celebration of what had already happened: the birth of the church at the moment of Jesus' Death on the Cross. For there, Jesus, reigning from the Tree on the crest of Calvary, provides for the nucleus of a Christian community: To Mary, keeping watch at the foot of the Cross, he says, "Woman, behold your son!" Then he said to John, "Behold your mother!" And the evangelist tells us, "And from that hour the disciple took her to his own home" (John 19:26–27).

In his words from the Cross, Jesus imparts the truth that the *ekklesia*, the community which calls together people of differing backgrounds, is predicated on a commitment to respect and care for each another. The Greek phrase *eis ta idia,* translated "into his own home," does not mean that John takes Mary into his physical dwelling place, but connotes instead that he shares with her his own possessions, and brings her into his circle of intimates. But recent evidence suggests that today, the church is running the risk of becoming something more akin to a "brood of vipers," that most damning of epithets hurled by John the Baptist at the religious community of his day (Matthew 3:7). In the Episcopal Church, whose most serious divisions were once described as "low and lazy, broad and hazy, high and crazy," we now find pitched camps: "orthodox" vs. "unorthodox"; liberal vs. conservative; biblical Christians vs. secular humanists. Words like "fundamentalist," "apostate," and "heretic"—long absent from the church's lexicon—are now being hurled by Christians at other Christians with what we used to call gay abandon.

Some years ago, I remember being riveted to my TV screen, absolutely mesmerized by a segment of *Sixty Minutes,* which introduced the viewing public to a revolutionary surgical procedure called induced hypothermia. A patient has an aneurism, a blood clot in the brain, which, should it burst, would result in the certain death of the patient. Conventional surgery is too delicate, because—if the doctor's scalpel is a millimeter off—the aneurism may burst,

. . . . . .

thereby bringing about the very occurrence the procedure was intended to prevent. Instead, the surgeons lower the body temperature to well below freezing, drain the body of its blood, open up the cranium, remove the aneurism safely, and then warm up the patient and put the blood back into the body! This is not science fiction. This is modern medicine! I believe there is a parable for us in this story. Perhaps the church needs to induce a spiritual hypothermia. We need to experience with Jesus the cold wood of the Cross. We need, like him, to empty ourselves, to rid ourselves of the offending aneurysms, boils, cysts, and tumors with which the Body of Christ is infected. And then we come to the Altar, to receive the Body and Blood of Christ, that great privilege of membership in the Christian community, and there offer our selves, our souls, and bodies to be a reasonable, holy, and living sacrifice. When we do that, it is as if we were receiving a transfusion. We are strengthened, energized, equipped for service in a renewed Christian community.

> Well might the sun in darkness hide, and shut its glories in;
> When God, the mighty maker, died, for His own creature's sin.
>
> Thus might I hide my blushing face while His dear cross appears;
> Dissolve my heart in thankfulness, and melt mine eyes to tears.
> >At the cross, at the cross, where I first saw the light,
> > And the burden of my heart rolled away;
> > It was there by faith, I received my sight,
> > And now I am happy all the day.

Isaac Watts, "Alas! And did my Savior bleed," *Lift Every Voice and Sing II,* No. 30

. . . . .

"Now the iron bars are broken, Christ from death to life is born"
—*The Hymnal 1982*, No. 191

IN JOHN'S RESURRECTION STORY, Jesus says to Mary Magdalene, "Do not cling to me" (John 20:17). Our Lord's words seem harsh at first. But what he is really telling Mary is that he did not come back through the door of her life to resume the old relationship of human fellowship. Rather, his resurrection opened up—as the great All Saints hymn describes it— "a yet more glorious day." There was therefore no need to hold on to a sentimental remembrance of his earthly existence. The Easter event means that we are joint partakers of a new realm of existence, "where," as the burial office reminds us, "sorrow and pain are no more, neither sighing but life everlasting." Sometimes, however, we deprive ourselves of participation in the joy of the Resurrection precisely because we cling to the wrong Jesus.

Some of us cling to a Jesus who is dead and gone. We must remember that Mary Magdalene could not find Jesus in the garden because she was looking for a corpse. Some of us still make the same mistake. Easters come and go, and we come to church and belt out, "Jesus lives, our hearts know well, naught from us his love shall sever"—and yet we carry on as if the only Christ we know was an itinerant preacher who lived in Palestine two thousand years ago.

Some of us cling to a Jesus whom we make into our own personal property. We come to church to make *our* communion. We wish the Peace had not been reintroduced into the service, because it reminds us that we are sharing the pew with others. We are concerned with working out *our* salvation. We "come to the garden *alone*." Such behavior is alien to Resurrection Christians. The joy of the Resurrection is not something we can keep to ourselves. At its very core, Christianity is the religion of the community. If we make Jesus into our private chaplain, our faith is seriously impaired.

. . . . . .

When I was in college, I had a rather unusual part-time job. I played the organ for Sunday morning services in the chapel of Her Majesty's Prison in Montreal. Father Mac—my mentor and parish priest from Brooklyn—had returned to his native Montreal as the prison's chaplain, and believed that such (volunteer) work would be good for my soul's health! Father Mac would visit me occasionally, and on one such occasion phoned ahead to give me a lesson in ethics. He was bringing to dinner a former inmate, but made it very clear that since "Greg" had paid his debt to society, it would be unethical of me to let on that I had known him as a prisoner. I assured my mentor that I understood perfectly. Over pre-dinner sherry, one of my classmates asked Greg how he had met Father McFarlane. "I met him on the outside," came the showstopping response. His frame of reference, despite his release, was still the inside of a cell.

"Stone walls do not a prison make/Nor iron bars a cage," wrote the poet. We live in a world inhabited by people who are spiritually imprisoned. Their life is a series of Good Fridays, and the joy of the Resurrection seems to them remote, elusive. It is to such a world that we are called to bring the good news of Christ's victory over the grave. But to achieve this, we must be Resurrection people, not Good Friday people. To achieve this, we must not cling to a Jesus fashioned of our own sentimentality, our own inadequacies, our own shortcomings, or our own convenience. Rather we must put our faith in him whom God has raised from the dead, "the Lamb that has been slain to receive power, and riches, and wisdom, and might, and honor, and glory, and blessing" (Revelation 5:12).

> *Now the iron bars are broken, Christ from death to life is born,*
> *glorious life, and life immortal, on his resurrection morn.*
> *Christ has triumphed, and we conquer by his mighty enterprise:*
> *we with him to life eternal by his resurrection rise.*

Christopher Wordsworth, "Alleluia, alleluia! Hearts and voices heavenward raise," *The Hymnal 1982*, No. 191

SEPARATING THE NAVE from the chancel in Calvary Church, Pittsburgh, is a magnificent rood screen, made of exquisitely carved oak. A rood screen is so named because on top of it is found a rood (an old English word for "cross"). Calvary's rood is a life-size depiction of the Crucifixion, with figures of our Lord's Mother and John, the beloved disciple, standing at its foot. If you inspect the other side the cross, however, you will discover intricate carvings of the Lamb of God and the symbols of the four Gospels. One's first reaction to it is that it's very ornate for the back of a cross. The reason is that it was, at one time, the front! Ralph Adams Cram, Calvary's architect, was an unabashed Anglo-Catholic, and he envisioned a traditional, suffering crucifix atop the rood screen, but the building committee rejected it for being just a little too "popish," and therefore offensive to many Protestant Episcopalians and all of their Presbyterian friends. So the Agnus Dei and the four evangelists sufficed for many years. Then, Dr. Cram had a brilliant idea, born of the spirit of Anglican compromise. Instead of a crucifix, he designed a Christus Rex—Christ the King a figure of Christ, crowned and in eucharistic vestments, reigning from the Cross, and not suffering on it. So Dr. Van Etten, the eighth rector of Calvary, commissioned the work, turned the cross around, and affixed to it this acceptable figure of our Lord, which has dominated Calvary's nave ever since. On the Feast of Christ the King (the last Sunday after Pentecost) we fix our gaze on that majestic figure, and pray that "the peoples of the earth, divided and enslaved by sin," might be "brought together under his most gracious rule."

It seems incongruous, at first, that the Gospel lesson for Christ the King is taken from Luke's account of the Crucifixion. But what can the convicted, suffering, dying Christ tell us about kingship? The answer is, "Everything." Jesus was in total control of the situation.

At this death he was surrounded by different groups of people—the rulers of the empire, the mockers, the blasphemous thief, those who gambled for his belongings. Though condemned, Jesus reigned over all of them from his place of execution. The Christus Rex, then, is but a theological translation of the Crucifix.

The funny thing is that majesty, ultimately, does not exist in ostensible power, but in weakness and vulnerability. Harun al-Rashid was the caliph of Baghdad, under whose rule the Eastern Caliphate reached the height of its splendor. But he is best known to us in the tales of *The Arabian Nights*, where in humble disguise he goes out at night from his palace to move unknown among his people. Queen Elizabeth the Queen Mother, who turned one hundred years old in the first year of the new century, is cherished and revered among Britons because she and her husband, George V, stayed in London during World War II, visited her subjects in the bombed-out East End, and even quaffed a pint in a local pub. Her daughter, conversely, it will be remembered, earned the derision of her subjects when she was her most regal and aloof, holed up at Balmoral Castle in the days after the death of the Princess of Wales. As a result, Buckingham Palace has retained the services of a public relations firm, in an attempt to make the Royal Family appear more approachable and down-to-earth.

When all is said and done, we worship in Jesus a paradoxical God—"King of Kings yet born of Mary" and "Lord of lords in human vesture." We worship the One who, St. Paul tells us in his letter to the Philippians, "though he was in the form of God, did not count equality with God a thing to be grasped, . . . but humbled himself and became obedient unto death, even death on a cross" (Philippians 2:6–8).

> *Crown him with many crowns, the Lamb upon his throne;*
> *Hark! How the heavenly anthem drowns   all music but its own;*
> *awake, my soul, and sing of him who died for thee,*
> *and hail him as thy matchless King through all eternity.*

Matthew Bridges, "Crown him with many crowns," *The Hymnal 1982*, No. 494

"O Love that wilt not let me go, I rest my weary soul in thee"

—*The Hymnal 1940*, No. 458

IF HOLLYWOOD TEACHES US anything at all about how we should express ourselves in loving relationships, it is that we should be spontaneous. Since "love conquers all"—when we are in love, Hollywood-style—all rules of propriety, social convention, and decorum go out the window. We don't care what people will say, think, or do; at worst they will be scandalized, at best they will indulge our spontaneity. Examples abound. In an old Grace Kelly film called *The Swan*, Miss Kelly plays a princess (appropriately enough) who falls in love with her brothers' tutor (Louis Jourdan). She leaves the ball with him and goes for a ride in a carriage. She then comes back, makes a public declaration of her love, and kisses the star-struck commoner in the presence of the crown prince, to whom her marriage had already been arranged.

The message from that other locus of opinion influence, Madison Avenue, is that expressions of love must be extravagant. The advertising industry tries to convince the middle-aged husband that, although his wife does indeed cherish the $5/_8$ carat diamond engagement ring he brought at great sacrifice while in graduate school, he is duty bound, now that he is a successful businessman, to lavish upon his faithful spouse a pair of stud earrings, weighing in, say, at two carats apiece.

In the twelfth chapter of St. John's Gospel, we read of a loving act which is both spontaneous and extravagant. Mary and Martha of Bethany host what amounts to a farewell testimonial for their friend Jesus. In the midst of the party, something shocking happens: "Mary brought a pound of costly perfume, oil of pure nard, and anointed the feet of Jesus, and wiped them with her hair." In that impulsive and emotional act were expressed profound gratitude, undying affection, and unbridled love. She knew there was no way that she could repay Jesus for restoring her brother, Lazarus, to life, but she intuitively felt the act could convey to Jesus what she felt in her heart. And in the same spirit as the widow who gave all that she had, Mary goes all out. Modern-day naysayers who criticize the church for allegedly shutting up their "bowels of compassion" (1 John 3:17 KJV) for the poor as it spends money, instead, on things of beauty, have their patron "saint" in Judas, who upbraids Mary for her costly act of worship.

But the question is more complex than it appears, for it speaks to the deeper issue of our response to God's love through our stewardship. If God is little more than a good-natured individual, a distant friend who helps to smooth out the rough places in life, he is unlikely to elicit any great outpouring of love. To those for whom God is little more than someone who makes something tolerable out of a rather hopeless world, God is deserving more of our sympathy than our worship. But if we rightly see God as incarnational, a God who, according to the Epistle to the Hebrews, has "been touched with the feeling of our infirmities," we feel compelled to worship such a God in spirit and in truth. Our instinctive response is to say, "All things are thine, no gift have we, Lord, of all gifts to offer thee." We learn from Mary of Bethany that worship of God is grounded in the love of God, and that that love can be costly and make us vulnerable. But we also know that love is liberating and infectious. We know that our love will spill over to our fellow pilgrims along the way, and that it can permeate the whole community of believers, much as Mary's perfume filled the house.

> *O Love, that wilt not let me go,*
> *I rest my weary soul in thee;*
> *I give thee back the life I owe,*
> *That in thine ocean depths its flow*
> *May richer, fuller be.*

George Matheson, "O Love that wilt not let me go," *The Hymnal 1940*, No. 458

· · · · · ·

"Our earthly rulers falter, our people drift and die"

—The Hymnal 1982, No. 591

WE ALL HAVE MET JUSTICE. Justice is portrayed in the statues, sculptures, and murals found in our nation's courtrooms. Justice is a woman. She is best depicted by that sex known as fairer, that half of humanity to whom characteristics such as charity, compassion, and empathy seem to come more naturally. Justice, as she presides in stony silence over trials and hearings, is arrayed with her attributes. In one hand, she holds the scales, on which she weighs the evidence. In her other hand, Justice wields a sword, with which she metes out any necessary punishment. But the most significant attribute of Justice is her blindfold. Justice, it is alleged, has no interest whatsoever in the identity of the perpetrator of a given deed. But we know that often the scales of Justice are weighted by such factors as the ability of the defendant to afford competent counsel. We know, too, that the sword of Justice is sometimes sharpened and at other times blunted when it comes to punishment. The punishment, with all due respects to Gilbert and Sullivan, does not fit the crime so much as it does the criminal. And, amazingly—although Justice is holding the scales with one hand and a sword in another—she somehow manages to lift her blindfold to peek at the defendant. We know all too well that, in the American system of jurisprudence, race, age, gender, and socioeconomic status are considerations not irrelevant to Justice.

Justice is a fundamental component in the Judeo-Christian tradition. As the source of all human justice, Jahweh demands that we practice it in our dealings with one another. The prophet Amos declares that "justice shall run down like waters, and righteousness like an ever-flowing stream." But we often forget the words that precede that famous verse: "Even though you offer me your burnt offerings and cereal offerings, I will not accept them. . . . Take away from me the noise of your songs; to the melody of your harps I will not listen"

· · · · · ·

(Amos 5:22–24). In other words, Amos is telling us that, unless we are doers of justice, all of our religiosity, all of our hymnody, all of our worship is for naught. All of us, both as individuals and as church, have, at one time or another, been deaf to the cries of the oppressed. We have been like the unnamed man in the parable (popularly known as "Dives," which is Latin for "rich man"), who fared sumptuously every day, ignoring the pleas of Lazarus, who had to be content with the crumbs that fell from the rich man's table. We have been like the priests and the Levites in the parable of the Good Samaritan, who walked on the other side of the road, refusing to stop and help the victim of a crime.

An unarmed black man, standing in his doorway, is shot to death by the police. A gay college student in Wyoming is strapped to a fence and left to die, for no other reason than his sexual orientation. Two high school classmates go on a rampage, killing a dozen of their fellow students and themselves. Such events make us listen anew to the words uttered nearly four decades ago by Martin Luther King, Jr., a lover and seeker of justice. When he accepted the Nobel Peace Prize, he said, "I refuse to accept the view that mankind is so tragically bound to the starless midnight of racism and war that the bright daybreak of peace and brotherhood can never become a reality. I believe that unarmed truth and unconditional love will have the final word in reality. This is why right temporarily defeated is stronger than evil triumphant." We pray for the day when justice will be more than the dream of Amos and Martin, but a reality in our land.

> *O God of earth and altar, bow down and hear our cry,*
> *our earthly rulers falter, our people drift and die;*
> *the walls of gold entomb us, the swords of scorn divide,*
> *take not thy thunder from us, but take away our pride.*
>
> Gilbert Keith Chesterton, "O God of earth and altar," *The Hymnal 1982*, No. 591

· · · · ·

"Thou art the potter, I am the clay"

—Lift Every Voice and Sing II, No. 145

WHATEVER HAPPENED TO FEAR? For those of us who are middle-aged or better, the element of fear was part and parcel of our upbringing. I grew up in a close-knit community, largely made up of West Indian immigrants, in Brooklyn, New York. Long before Hillary Rodham Clinton, that community took seriously the idea that it takes a village to raise a child. A little boy who had done something he ought not be doing, two or three blocks from home, returned home in dread fear because he knew that one of his surrogate mothers (who had discovered him *in flagrante delicto*) would have telephoned his resident mother with news of his misdeed long before he was able to reach his doorstep. On *Father Knows Best*, when Bud's negligence put a dent in the car, or Betty's prom dress put a dent in the family budget, Jane Wyman would wag her finger with the threat: "Wait till your father gets home." The message reached us loud and clear that there were consequences for our actions. This all predates, of course, the contemporary notion that the parent/child relationship should be characterized first and foremost by friendship.

Fear is no longer a staple of Christianity. We no longer fear that our transgressions will cause us to be drummed out of its fellowship. In an article in *The New Yorker* entitled "The Future of Faith: Confessions of a Churchgoer," John Updike comments: "In its centuries of dominance, [the church] had the power to exclude and excommunicate; now, unlike most other organizations, it will take us if we so much as show up." Mr. Updike makes a similar statement about the absence of even a vestige of fire and brimstone from the pulpit, characterizing the tone of certain contemporary sermons as "laid-back." "A certain pleasantly faded flower-child, hug-your-neighbor sweetness," he observes, " has replaced the sterner old dispensations." The word "fear" seems to have been excised from the 1979 Book of

. . . . . .

Common Prayer. No longer, for example, do we enter marriage "reverently, discreetly, advisedly, soberly, and in the fear of God."

"Fear" has gotten a bum rap. We learned that "the fear of God is the beginning of wisdom." We recited in the *Magnificat*, "His mercy is on them that fear him throughout all generations." Not that long ago, "God-fearing" was an adjective that was often coupled with "upright" or "respectable." Now to be afraid of anything is to be a wimp. Many of us, as schoolchildren, learned William Ernest Henley's "Invictus," which begins

> *Out of the night that covers me,*
> *Dark as a pit from pole to pole,*
> *I thank whatever gods may be*
> *For my inconquerable soul*

and which ends with that great paean to self:

> *I am the master of my fate,*
> *I am the captain of my soul*

Good poetry, bad theology! We would do well to put things in proper perspective again. The hymnwriter seems to have gotten it right:

> *Have thine own way, Lord, have thine own way,*
> *Thou art the potter, I am the clay.*
> *Mold me and melt me after thy will,*
> *While I am waiting, yielded and still.*

Adelaide A. Pollard, "Have thine own way, Lord," *Lift Every Voice and Sing II*, No. 145

"Send forth, O Lord, thy strong Evangel by many messengers, all hearts to win"
—*The Hymnal 1982*, No. 540

WHILE SERVING THE CHURCH in the Congo as a seminary professor, I would often preach in rural congregations in that country and in neighboring Rwanda. Since French was understood only by the small fraction of church members who were formally educated, my sermons were translated, usually by a catechist, into the local language. The Holy Eucharist was also celebrated in the local language "understanded of the people," but despite my lack of familiarity with it, I knew exactly where I was in the service. Liturgical appointments and practices deemed normative and even essential in First World countries were absent from the worship of the people of God in Rwandan villages, but—to borrow a phrase from the great Anglican liturgist Dom Gregory Dix—"the shape of the liturgy" was intact. Theology, too, was indigenized. Ancestor worship, which missionaries a century ago might have denounced as pagan, was seen as but a variation of the doctrine of Communion of the Saints.

In one of his epistles, Paul proclaims that he has "become all things to all men" (1 Corinthians 9:22). Often taken out of context, the phrase has, unfortunately, come to mean that its utterer has no backbone, no identity, and worse, no integrity. Such a wishy-washy person goes along with the crowd, accommodating himself to opinions that prevail at the moment. His views on any given topic are remarkably similar to those of the last person he spoke to. But such an interpretation is not what the Blessed Apostle had in mind. He simply meant that, in order to win souls for Christ, we must present the Gospel in ways intelligible to the "target" audience.

Perhaps we should reconsider the reputation of the lowly creature called the chameleon, a lizard-like animal who has the ability to blend into whatever environment he happens to enter. He can, for example, change his color to that of the leaf on which he is resting so that he becomes virtually invisible to his predator. Changeability, to the chameleon, is a survival technique. It enables him to flourish and, moreover, to be of service by, for example, controlling the insect population. And yet the poor chameleon has been maligned. To be described as a chameleon is to be labeled as someone who just goes along with the program in order to curry the favor of others.

The church and her ministers are at their best when they are chameleons, able, like Paul, to become one with the local terrain. Chameleon-like adaptability is not only advisable; it is essential if the church is to flourish and be effective. Conversely, the church is at its worst when her leaders interpret Paul's words to mean that they should say one thing to one group, and something else to another group, or when they choose words because they are expedient at the moment. The church is least effective, and indeed loses her credibility, when the Gospel message is crafted with an aim to please hearers and not challenge them. The church instead must be guided by the words of the prophet Ezekiel: "Whether they hear or refuse to hear, they will know that a prophet has been among them."

> *Send forth, O Lord, thy strong Evangel*
> *by many messengers, all hearts to win;*
> *make haste to help us in our weakness;*
> *break down the realm of Satan, death, and sin:*
> *the circle of the earth shall then proclaim*
> *thy kingdom, and the glory of thy Name.*

Karl Heinrich von Bogatzky, trans. Charles Winfred Douglas and Arthur William Farlander, "Awake, thou Spirit of the watchmen," *The Hymnal 1982*, No. 540

. . . . . .

"Prayer is the soul's sincere desire, unuttered or expressed"

—*The Hymnal 1940,* No. 419

THE IMPORTUNATE WIDOW in the eighteenth chapter of Luke was not merely a woman whose husband had died; she was the very emblem of poverty and hopelessness. In this parable, the widow had an enemy referred to only as her "adversary" or "opponent," against whom—in the patriarchal society of biblical Palestine—she was totally defenseless. Hoping for protection, she went frequently before the city's judge to plead her case, but she had no resources—no money, no influence, no clout—with which to influence him. But she did have one thing, and she used it; that was persistence. She hung in there; she wouldn't quit; she didn't take "no" for an answer. We can imagine that every morning, when the judge arrived at his chambers, the widow was sitting on his steps, waiting for him, pleading her case, the details of which the judge came to know by heart! He refused her at first, but after a while, he said to himself, "Though I neither fear God nor regard man, yet because this widow bothers me, I will vindicate her, or else she will wear me out by her continual coming." So the powerless, helpless, friendless widow won the day on account of her determination. She got what was due her because of her perseverance.

The oppressed in our own day have taken a page from the widow's book. Civil rights legislation in this country was not enacted because America woke up one morning with a guilty conscience. Laws changed because people marched, picketed, protested, and took part in sit-ins. Racial minority groups won the inalienable rights granted to others in the Declaration of Independence two centuries earlier because people subjected themselves to being attacked by dogs, kicked, hosed, beaten, and even killed. Such equality as women enjoy in the workplace did not come about because sexism and male chauvinism died of natural

· · · · ·

causes. Women have had to undertake the re-education of men—whether husbands, fathers, sons, employers, employees, or colleagues—in order to change their attitudes.

But Jesus told this story to teach his disciples how to pray, "that they ought always to pray and not to lose heart." Jesus would have us rise above the infantile approach in which we use prayer as a bludgeon, forcing God to meet our expectations. Jesus would entreat us not to despair when our first attempt at prayer does not yield the desired results. Jesus would have us understand that prayer is work. "The prayers of the righteous availeth much" (James 5:16), not because prayer is magic, but because prayer inspires us, empowers us to get off our knees and put our prayer into action. The widow could have abandoned her post and given up her cause, but—knowing that it was just—she translated her prayer into action and staged a sit-in at the judge's chambers. To pray and not to lose heart is to carry out the mandate of our baptismal covenant to "strive for justice and peace among all people, and respect the dignity of every human being."

> *Prayer is the soul's sincere desire,*
> *Unuttered or expressed,*
> *The motion of a hidden fire*
> *That trembles in the breast.*
> *Prayer is the burden of a sigh*
> *The falling of a tear,*
> *The upward glancing of an eye*
> *When none but God is near.*

James Montgomery, "Prayer is the soul's sincere desire," *The Hymnal 1940*, No. 419

. . . . . .

"O feed me, Lord, that I may feed thy hungering ones with manna sweet"
—The Hymnal 1940, No. 574

WHEN WE READ a miracle story in the Bible, the question that we find ourselves asking is, "Is it true?" or "Did it really happen?" Peter Gomes, in his book *Sermons: Biblical Wisdom for Daily Living* (he is also author of *The Good Book: Reading the Bible with Mind and Heart*) makes a radical suggestion. He writes "The question to be put about a miracle is not 'Is it true?' or even 'How can this be?' but rather 'What does this say?' At its essence a miracle is a message—an illustration or demonstration of a message that God chooses to communicate to us. A miracle is God's extraordinary message in the midst of the ordinary."

We who like to think of ourselves as erudite, savvy, and urbane churchgoers pride ourselves nowadays on our intellectual acumen. We remind ourselves that we don't have to leave our brains at the door when we come to church. Nothing escapes our intellectual curiosity. But sometimes we can overdo it. If we read Scripture carefully, we can take a clue from the reactions of those for whom miracles are performed. When they saw the star in the eastern sky, the shepherds didn't say to each other, "Do you think the star is really there, or is it just some rare meteorological occurrence?" They just followed the star to the manger. The man cured of his blindness did not inquire into the ophthalmological methods of the Great Physician; he just shared with the world the fact that he could see. The people at the wedding reception in Cana didn't ask how Jesus managed to change the water into wine; they just commented on the fact that the vintage Merlot was a lot better than the jug wine the host had been serving up to that point. In the feeding of the five thousand, the multitudes didn't ask, "Where did all this food come from?" Instead, they said, "This is indeed the prophet who is to come into the world." While it is true that every miracle has in it some element of the manifestation of power, as well as what we might call the suspension of the laws of nature, a miracle, when all is said and done, is a message from God to us. It is a response to a need. It is an answer to a prayer.

We are especially tempted to spiritualize the story of the miraculous feeding of the multitudes (John 6:1–15). Because we see in it a foreshadowing of the Eucharist, we can look at the loaves and fishes as symbols of a deeper spiritual refreshment. In fact, if we read on in St. John's Gospel, Jesus seems to reinforce this idea in our heads. He warns us not to go after the bread that perishes like manna in the wilderness, but that we should seek instead food that endures. But the fact remains that Jesus did, in fact, address the basic need of the crowd—their physical hunger. Jesus did not appoint a committee or launch a war on poverty. He did not convene a panel of experts or bring in a consultant. There were no slick posters with catchy phrases. He just sat the people down and fed them. Jesus knew that the people had both physical and spiritual hunger, but that they could not really hear the message of the Gospel until their physical hunger was dealt with. The miracle of the Feeding of the Five Thousand is that God is willing to provide not only bread, but the Bread of Life.

Now that we know the secret of miracles, we don't have to sit around waiting for a Red Sea to part. If we understand that a miracle is a sign, an answer to a prayer, a message of God's love, it occurs to us at once that we all can be miracle workers. We perform a miracle when we visit homebound parishioners and bring the assurance that the church has not forgotten them. We perform a miracle when we spend time with members of our own family (who are all too often the ones we neglect most). We perform a miracle when we resist the ever-present temptation to be "clubby," and show hospitality to newcomers to our churches.

> Let us pray:
> *O lead me, Lord, that I may lead*
>   *The wandering, and the wavering feet:*
>
>   . . . . . .

O feed me, Lord, that I may feed
Thy hungering ones with manna sweet.

O strengthen me, that while I stand
Firm on the Rock, and strong in thee,
I may stretch out a loving hand
To wrestlers with the troubled sea.

O teach me, Lord, that I may teach
The precious things thou dost impart;
And wing my words, that they may reach
The hidden depths of many a heart.

Frances Ridley Havergal, "Lord, speak to me," *The Hymnal 1940*, No. 574

. . . . . .

"Let goods and kindred go"

—The Hymnal 1982, No. 687

THERE WAS AN ARTICLE in *The New York Times* about one of the Holy Father's visits to Mexico. Its headline jumped out from the page at me: "Pope Urges Bishops to Minister to the Rich." "Love for the poor must be preferential, but not exclusive," John Paul II said in an apostolic exhortation. "The leading sectors of society have been neglected and many people have thus been estranged from the church." Needless to say, thousands of Episcopalians, reached for comment "in church, or in trains, or in shops, or at tea" (*The Hymnal 1982*, No. 293), in a sudden burst of ecumenical spirit, enthusiastically welcomed the papal decree. Whether wielding croquet mallets or consuming watercress sandwiches (crusts removed, of course), they all agreed that the Pope's proclamation might just possibly set in motion a long overdue reversal of the tide. "At last, somebody is thinking about us," they proclaimed. "Now, perhaps maligning us will cease to be the odds-on favorite sport of preachers!"

And Lord knows, preachers have no dearth of material. Those who would bash the rich find supportive texts on almost every page of Scripture. The camel will squeeze through the eye of a needle with less difficulty than it takes for the rich man to enter heaven (Mark 10:25). In one parable, the rich man and the poor Lazarus undergo a kind of Eddie Murphy/Dan Ackroydesque "trading places," with the rich man spending eternity in torment of unquenchable fire and Lazarus enjoying the comfort of Abraham's bosom (Luke 16:19–23). Even when our Lady sings Magnificat, she delivers the walloping message that "the rich will be sent empty away" (Luke 1:53). And in his encounter with the rich young ruler, Jesus startles him by telling him that a prescription for eternal life entails giving up all that he possesses (Mark 10:21).

· · · · · ·

Now the reason that the Bible is the all-time bestseller is that it predates Freud. It appeals to us because we find in its pages our families, friends, neighbors, and, if we are honest, ourselves. The rich young ruler is a case in point. Like many of us, he is eager to be of service. He comes running to Jesus. He figures a little buttering up won't hurt, so he genuflects and calls Jesus "good teacher." But he gives himself away by his question: "What must I *do* to inherit eternal life?" Then as now there was a perception that salvation could be obtained by doing an act or series of acts. A healthy body is obtained by proper diet and exercise; an education is obtained through study and passing exams. But not so salvation. There must be an inwardness of character that springs from one's relation to God in the first place. God is not Santa Claus, who rewards us for being either naughty or nice. Religion is not a heavenly insurance policy, for which the premiums are church attendance and good works. This is why Jesus, while moved that the young man observed the law, nevertheless informed him that he still lacked something.

Jesus' advice was tailor-made for the rich young ruler. Jesus could see at once that the young man's millions would be a hindrance to discipleship. The other disciples had left their livelihoods—James and John even left their father, Zebedee, with a net full of holes—to follow Jesus. They were willing to "let goods and kindred go." While they were about the business of assisting Jesus in healing the sick, raising the dead, and ushering in the kingdom, they just didn't have time to wait for the rich young man to take his cell phone out of his knapsack and call his broker, or worry them to death that he couldn't find *The Wall Street Journal* in some sleepy little Palestinian village. His possessions, therefore, would be a hindrance to his ministry. So the young man, having come running to Jesus, went away slowly and sorrowfully.

But there is also in the Master's words generic advice for all of us who profess and call ourselves Christians. We need to get beyond seeking our own self-fulfillment. We must instead be motivated by loyalty to Christ and service to others, and then be willing to rid ourselves of whatever "baggage" we have. Upon closer examination, then, Scripture does not bash the rich for being rich. The problem, almost always, is the attitude the rich bring to their money, or the use to which they put it, or do not put it. The sin of the rich man in the parable was not his wealth but his depraved indifference to the poor man, Lazarus, at his gate. The rich are "sent empty away" not because they are rich but because they do not use their riches to alleviate the oppression of the poor. And if indeed, as some commentators believe, the eye of a needle is the arched gateway to a walled city through which the camel had to contort himself and perhaps go down on all fours so that his hump could clear the opening, then admission to heaven for the rich is not an impossibility, but it does take just a little more effort.

> *Let goods and kindred go,*
> *this mortal life also;*
> *The body they may kill:*
> *God's truth abideth still,*
> > *his kingdom is for ever.*

Martin Luther, "A mighty fortress is our God," *The Hymnal 1982*, No. 687

> *"I once was lost but now am found, was blind, but now I see"*
>
> —*The Hymnal 1982*, No. 671

EVERYBODY IN THE STORY of the miraculous healing of the man born blind (John 9) seems to have a special interest in him. To the disciples, the blind man's infirmity is a punishment. To the townspeople, the formerly blind man who had stood on the corner begging can no longer qualify as their object of pity and derision. The Pharisees take an interest in him because they hope to prove Jesus a fraud because he healed the man on the Sabbath. The man's parents claim to be clueless as to how it is that he now sees, or who is responsible for the miracle. Besides, they add, their son has reached his majority. Queries should be directed to him. And this is exactly what happens. But in the dialogue between the healed man and the Pharisees, two different languages are spoken. The formerly blind man speaks the unvarnished truth (if tinged with sarcasm) while the Pharisees resort to philosophical and theological discourse. They pull rank, and claim superiority based on the fact that they are disciples of Moses, and finally run the poor man out of town. Jesus, when he hears of this, seeks out the man, who discovers as a consequence that his newfound sight also enables him to believe in the Son of Man. Then Jesus has an encounter with the Pharisees, who say to him, "Are we also blind?" Jesus responds, "if you were blind, you would have no guilt, but now that you say, 'We see,' your guilt remains."

Clearly, the blind to Jesus are not just those whose physical vision is impaired. Jesus is referring to those whom the hymnwriter calls the "inly blind," those whose sight Jesus promises to restore when he preaches his inaugural sermon at Nazareth. Conversely, the self-righteous know-it-alls who claim that they see, the ones who have all the answers, are, according to Jesus, the ones who blind themselves to the truth of the Gospel.

Perhaps this miracle story is a parable for our times. We are knowledgeable, sophisticated, erudite. Our high technology makes it possible for us to accomplish things unimaginable even a generation ago. We can, for example, pick up the phone, say "office," and be connected to our place of employment. We can jump on the Concorde in London and arrive in New York before we left. And yet, hate crimes are on the rise, making people vulnerable to attack simply because of the color of their skin or their sexual orientation. And in our nation's cities, it seems to be increasingly dangerous to be caught "driving (or even breathing) while black." Those who claim to see and yet blind themselves to the truth of the Gospel exist, indeed, flourish, even in the bosom of the church. Some churchgoing folk—believing themselves to have a corner on the market of salvation and convinced that God has spoken only to them—create impenetrable spiritual ghettoes, with a jargon only its inhabitants can understand. Clearly they never heard the words of William Temple, Archbishop of Canterbury in the early forties, who said that the church is the only organization that exists primarily for the benefit of those *not* its members.

Kathleen Norris, in her book, *Amazing Grace,* writes that her most important breakthrough with regard to belief came not when she thought she had all the answers, but when she "learned to be as consciously skeptical and questioning of my disbelief and my doubts as I was of my burgeoning faith. This new perspective," she continues, "also helped me to deal with my anger over the fact that churches, as institutions so often behave in polarizing ways." Ms. Norris admits that she has, like most of us, inherited a pharisaical blindness, if for no other reason than that it gives us at least a fleeting sense of security. She relates that she has a kindred theological spirit with an Anglican monk who wrote that there must be room in our prayer life "for simultaneous contradictions" and "the sacredness of living in tensions." Jesus diagnoses the Pharisees' blindness. If we are honest, we must ask to what extent the diagnosis is also ours.

> *Amazing grace! how sweet the sound, that saved a wretch like me!*
> *I once was lost but now am found, was blind but now I see.*

John Newton, "Amazing grace," The Hymnal 1982, No. 671

. . . . . .

"Look not on the misusings of our grace"

—*The Hymnal 1982*, No. 337

IN THE EIGHTEENTH CHAPTER of St. Matthew's Gospel, Jesus tells a parable. A servant of the king is brought before his monarch and convicted of owing an unimaginably huge sum. When the king figures out that the servant cannot possibly pay the debt, he commands that the man, along with his wife and children, be sold into slavery—tantamount to a life sentence. When the servant hears the sentence, he throws himself on the mercy of the court, and this act of desperation moves the king to show mercy. He wipes out the entire debt as a sovereign act of grace, and the servant goes free. Unfortunately, while the master's mercy changes the servant's situation, it does not change his heart. No sooner is he out of the royal presence than he comes upon a fellow servant who owes him a comparative pittance. Although this second servant pleads with the first for the opportunity to repay the debt— even using the very words our recently pardoned friend used when the shoe was on the other foot—the servant who is owed the pittance is merciless toward his debtor. He even grabs his fellow servant by the throat, and then throws him into jail. When the king gets wind of this, he reverses his decision and delivers the wicked servant to the torturers.

You see, we cannot, as Christians, win God's forgiveness, but we can certainly lose it. We exist as a Christian community because of an act of mercy—Jesus' death on the Cross—and because of that fact, we are duty bound to exhibit such mercy to others. But as we look around, it would appear that we haven't quite mastered this lesson. Our willingness to forgive is just part and parcel of human nature, isn't it? And since it is, maybe a few suggestions are in order to help us follow the example of the wicked servant in the parable.

First, only forgive those people whom you like. Make sure your forgiveness is selective. Make allowances for the egregious transgressions of your friends, but be unstinting in decrying the peccadillos of your enemies. Make sure that your attitude toward drug use and the punishment for it depends on whether the user is a Presidential candidate or an inner-city youth.

Second, set an arbitrary limit to the number of times you forgive. Like Peter, who figured that seven times was plenty, calculate and nitpick. Set yourself up as judge and jury.

Third, despite the blessings that God has bestowed on you, make sure to begrudge others when they possess even a fraction of those blessings. Rail against affirmative action policies. Refuse to understand that they are but attempts to level the playing field, which, if level in the first place, would have made affirmative action unnecessary. Condemn everybody on welfare, and conveniently forget the fact that welfare exists for the rich in the form of a tax structure far more favorable to the haves than the have-nots.

Fourth, give the church five dollars a week when you pull down a hundred thousand a year. Justify your pittance by choosing one of the following excuses: a) It pays for the coffee I consume at coffee hour; b) It will keep my name on the parish rolls; c) Let the really rich people (dead or alive) pay the bills.

Finally, and most important, repeat over and over again, "I will forgive, but I'll never forget." Make sure, when you mouth words of absolution to your spouse, your child, or fellow parishioners that, deep down, you harbor the memory of the sin. Remember every jot and tittle of it so that, at some opportune time, you can throw it in the offender's face.

> *Look Father, look on his anointed face, and only look on us as found in him;*
> *look not on our misusings of thy grace, our prayer so languid, and our faith so dim:*
> *for lo! between our sins and their reward, we set the passion of thy Son our Lord.*
>
> William Bright, "And now, O Father, mindful of the love," *The Hymnal 1982*, No. 337

> *"Are we weak and heavy laden, cumbered with a load of care?"*
> —*Lift Every Voice and Sing II*, No. 109

WHEN WE HEAR THE WORD "baggage" nowadays, chances are we're not talking about those articles crafted by Samsonite, American Tourister, or Hartmann that we entrust to the airlines (even as we offer up a prayer that some day we will be reunited with them). No, we usually speak of baggage metaphorically—as a hindrance. A new job or a second marriage is doomed, we hear, because an individual carries too much baggage into the new relationship. Cicero, Ovid *et al.* were on the right track; the Latin word for "baggage" is *impedimenta*, literally, things that weigh you down.

The tenth chapter of Luke contains lessons from what could be called "Jesus' Handbook for Discipleship." In it, he admonishes his disciples that in order to be effective they must shed several kinds of baggage. The first kind of baggage is personal—no extra clothes, no purse, no sandals. Every time I read this lesson, it reminds me of my first trip to Europe more than thirty years ago when I met my high school classmate in Paris to begin a month of impecunious hitchhiking. When my friend took one look at the wardrobe I had packed (which included, as I remember, twenty-one shirts) he quickly removed about seventy-five percent of my *impedimenta*, and shipped back everything that wouldn't fit in a backpack! The second kind of baggage that Jesus tells his disciples to be rid of is societal baggage. They were to eschew elaborate greetings and eat what was put before them, even if it wasn't kosher. But the greatest baggage of them all was psychological baggage: he told them—if they are not received in a town—to shake the dust off their feet and move on.

Dust may seem insignificant compared to tunics, knapsacks, and leather sandals. But if not shaken off after each journey, dust becomes crusty, making it necessary to scrape it off.

Worse, in the rainy season, it will turn to mud in which the traveler will become bogged down. Likewise, even we Christians can become bogged down in our ill feelings, our grudges, our disappointments, and our rejections. All too often, we insist on weighing ourselves down with them, carrying them from place to place, from relationship to relationship, from parish to parish, from year to year. We will do well if we add to life's lessons the importance of traveling light.

> *Are we weak and heavy laden,*
> > *Cumbered with a load of care?*
> *Precious Savior, still our refuge,*
> > *Take it to the Lord in Prayer.*
> *Do thy friends despise, forsake thee?*
> > *Take it to the Lord in prayer.*
> *In his arms He'll take and shield thee,*
> > *Thou wilt find a solace there.*
>
> Joseph Scriven, "What a friend we have in Jesus," *Lift Every Voice and Sing II*, No. 109

> *"Come labor on, who dares stand idle on the harvest plain?"*
>
> —*The Hymnal 1982*, No. 541

THOSE WHO WOULD ADVOCATE for the immediate and total abolition of welfare have a biblical text on which to base their beliefs. St. Paul writes, "If anyone will not work, let him not eat" (2 Thessalonians 3:10). Paul even goes on to say that those living in idleness should be shunned. "If anyone refuses to obey what we say in this letter," he writes, "note that man, and have nothing to do with him, that he may be ashamed." Snobs in our congregations who have nothing to do with people who are beneath their dignity, or are from the other side of the tracks, now have biblical justification for their behavior. Ah, music to our elitist ears! The snubbing we have been doing all along is the same as making people ashamed, isn't it? Now there's a good reason for defining outreach as "keeping others out of our reach." Good ol' Paul!

Hermeneutics, from the Greek word for interpretation, is a branch of biblical theology that arises out of awareness of the ambiguity of the sacred text. It treats the problems inherent in attempting to interpret a text to mean the same thing today as it did when it was first written. It addresses the difficulties that occur when readers of the Bible ignore the context (time, culture, mores) in which the author wrote. Most hermeneuticians would agree, for example, that Paul's admonition that women should wear hats in church (2 Corinthians 11:10–16) is a culturally conditioned statement. In the Thessalonians passage, the hermeneutic exercise in which we must engage is more contextual. There was a belief among the inhabitants of Thessalonica that they had "arrived," theologically speaking; they were already saved; the *parousia* had come. Consequently, there was no need to work, since work, after all, was part of the curse inflicted upon Adam because of his fall from grace (Genesis 3:19). Like groups of Christians in every age, the Thessalonians had fallen prey to the foolish notion that concern about spiritual matters made it permissible for them to be casual about more mundane obligations, like work. Perhaps we know people like that who are so "religious," so heavenly minded, that they are of no earthly good!

Paul is saying that there is a practical side to religion. He would suggest that being devout does not mean being so caught up in other-worldliness that we live by the credo, "The Lord will provide." Devotion entails responsibility, being our Lord's hands and feet, assisting him in the building up of the kingdom. Each of us must pull his or her weight. Far from setting up a dichotomy between good-guy Christians and bad-guy welfare recipients, Jesus is saying that the bad guys are really those within the Christian community who are, as it were, the drones in the congregational hive, living off the industry of others. Worse, he points out, having fallen into idleness, their energies are channeled into meddlesome behavior, making themselves busybodies, who not only do not advance but actively hinder the church's mission. (Has Paul been snooping around our parishes?)

Before we condemn the idle whose unemployment may well be the result of economic injustice, let us take a look at those even within the bosom of the church whose idleness cannot be attributed to poverty, but who do precious little to promote the cause of the Gospel. The church, ever guided by the overarching ethic of Christian love, must continue to minister in Christ's name to all who are "the victims of hunger, fear, injustice, and oppression."

> *Come, labor on.*
> *Who dares stand idles on the harvest plain,*
> *while all around us waves the golden grain?*
> *And to each servant does the Master say,*
> *"Go work today."*

Jane Laurie Borthwick, "Come labor on," The Hymnal 1982, No. 541

"Blest are the pure in heart, for they shall see our God"

—The Hymnal 1982, No. 656

SOMEONE ONCE SAID of the Beatitudes that no other speech in the history of humankind has been so widely acclaimed yet so universally ignored. It may have been all right for those folk on a Galilean hillside, they say, but they just won't cut it today, in a world in which the revised golden rule holds sway: "Do unto others before they do unto you." Indeed, someone has suggested that twenty-first century Beatitudes would begin something like this: "Blessed are the rich, for they shall call the shots. Blessed are those who play it safe, for they shall get over." But the Beatitudes cannot be dismissed simply because they are difficult. They constitute, as do other utterances of our Lord, "an hard saying." They are nothing less than the charter for the Christian life. They are the law of the new kingdom that Jesus ushers in. The Beatitudes are not promises of the "sweet bye-and-bye." Nor are they the terms of some celestial insurance policy, which we cash in "when we tread the verge of Jordan" (*The Hymnal 1982*, No. 690). They are, instead, rules which, if followed, will ensure that we shall have life and have it abundantly.

We must know that we are poor (poor in the sense that we must come to grips with our need for God). We understand meekness if we know that the word translated as "meek" is also encountered in a verse from Matthew: "Take your yoke upon you and learn of me, for I am *gentle* and humble of heart." It is the same word which we encounter in the prophecy of Zechariah: "Behold, your king is coming to you, *meek*, and mounted on an ass." Meekness does not connote self-effacement or low self-esteem. It has more to do with the fact that self-confidence means we do not have to threaten, cajole, or demean to be effective. And I think Jesus was really on to something when he said that the persecuted are blessed. A history of persecution is not necessarily a bad thing. It can allow us to be sympathetic to those who suffer for whatever reason. It allows us to face adversity more readily. Sarah and Bessie Delaney, daughters of Suffragan Bishop for Colored Work Henry B. Delaney, wrote the book, *Having Our Say*, when they were both over one hundred years old; they relate that, after the 1929 stock market crash, those people who jumped out of windows on Wall Street were those who had known no adversity, and who thought that prosperity was their due. Poverty and ruin were alien to them, and—unable to come to grips with such a turn of events—they found the nearest window ledge. The sisters relate that people in Harlem, on the other hand, although affected even more adversely by the economic turn of events, saw the crash as "just another crisis." They were able to pick up the pieces and regroup. Being able, as St. Paul tells us, to "know how to be exalted and how to be abased" is a blessing. It makes us more effective when we reach out to others, because we've "been there, done that." We become, as the Dutch theologian Henri Nouwen described it, "wounded healers."

More and more people are getting in touch with poverty, meekness, mournfulness, and persecution as they discover "spirituality." Nowadays you can even get a Ph.D. in spirituality. But bear in mind that "victims of poverty, fear, injustice, and oppression" have been earning honorary degrees in that subject for centuries. It is no coincidence, for example, that the songs of some of those people are called "spirituals." They, too, speak poignantly to the human condition, and resonate with the Beatitudes, those words which Jesus presented to his hearers as a new paradigm for Christian conduct.

> *Blest are the pure in heart,*
> *for they shall see our God;*
> *the secret of the Lord is theirs,*
> *their soul is Christ's abode.*

John Keble, "Blest are the pure in heart," *The Hymnal 1982*, No. 656

"Manifest in making whole palsied limbs and fainting soul"

—The Hymnal 1982, No. 135

WHEN I USED TO COMMUTE from Connecticut to my office at the national church head-quarters in New York City, I passed through Grand Central Terminal every morning and evening. Grand Central is a study in contrasts. The casual observer will see only an army of well-clad, scurrying commuters, designer briefcases in hand—the yuppies, the corporate giants, the movers and shakers of Wall Street and Madison Avenue. But there was another world in a room of magnificent proportions just to the south of the main hall. The words etched in marble over its arched entrance tell us that it was called "The Waiting Room." For the people here, Grand Central is their home. They are in rags, not designer clothes. They carry their worldly goods in shopping bags. The waiting room's denizens are the homeless, the forgotten, the underclass. They are sprawled out on what were once elegant benches, which look not unlike pews in a church. These are the addicted and afflicted, the jetsam and flotsam of society.

The pool at Bethesda (John 5:2–18) was perhaps the biblical equivalent of the waiting room at Grand Central. It was in fact an ancient Roman bath. Long before Christ, toga-clad citizens came here for their ablutions. But by the time of Christ, it had become the derelict haunt for the halt, the lame, the crippled, the leprous. They passed their time here, day in and day out, in their misery. But they lived in hope of a cure. The pool was fed by a natural spring, and once a day when the spring erupted, it caused the waters of the pool to be disturbed. It was a pious belief of the Jews that the disturbance was caused by an angel, and the Jews further believed that anyone suffering from any kind of infirmity could be cured if he were the first to step into the water after the turbulence. Into this depressing scene steps

Jesus. He scans the crowd and picks out its most piteous member, a man who had been sick for thirty-eight years, much of that time probably spent lying there in misery, just out of reach of the healing pool. Jesus asks what seems to be a silly question: "Do you want to be healed?" The paralytic's response is not a resounding "yes," as we would expect, but a long series of excuses and complaints, about how each day—perhaps as many as 14,000 of them—when someone carries him to the pool, somebody else beats him to the punch. Jesus' question was not so silly after all. For good reason does he ask the paralytic if it is his *will* to get better: perhaps the paralytic thinks he has a good thing going—a shaded spot, friends to commiserate with, enough food to keep body and soul together; perhaps he knows that, once healed, once hale and hearty, he will have to make an honest man of himself; he would have to earn a living!

Do we want to be healed? So often, like the cripple man at the pool, we who are on our Christian pilgrimage opt for the excuse; opt for the time-honored practice of projection. It is always far easier to blame someone else for our lot in life. Ever since Mary and Martha complained to Jesus: "If you had been here, our brother would not have died," we find it all too convenient to pass the buck. "If only I had had a more caring husband, I would be better off," proclaims the wronged wife. "If my children hadn't worn me out, I'd be in better shape," laments the put-upon father. It is easier for the black person to lay blame at the door of the racist society, or for the woman to cite the world's endemic sexism, than for either to acknowledge the fact that there is at least the possibility that he or she has been part of the problem. Does this nation want to be healed? The rash of murders in our nation's schools (in one case, both perpetrator and victim were six years old!) is explained away in terms of their parents' indifference or poverty or economic privation. But these are symptoms of a deeper malaise for which we all share part of the blame, a disease which, if cured, might mean that we have to take a greater responsibility for instilling values in our children. We

· · · · · ·

might just have to stop enjoying the fruits of our conspicuous consumerism long enough to work to improve the quality of life in our families and communities. Do we want to be healed?

> *Manifest in making whole*
> *palsied limbs and fainting soul;*
> *manifest in valiant fight,*
> *quelling all the devil's might;*
> *manifest in gracious will,*
> *ever bringing good from ill;*
> *anthems be to thee addressed,*
> *God in man made manifest.*

Christopher Wordsworth, "Songs of thankfulness and praise," *The Hymnal 1982*, No. 135

. . . . . .

"Jesus, thou divine Companion, help us all to work our best"

—The Hymnal 1982, No. 586

A FEW YEARS AGO, there was an article in *The New York Times Magazine* entitled "Hawks on Fifth." But it had nothing to do with warmongers. It had simply to do with the feathered variety: a family of one well-known species that had found a nesting place on the ledge of an apartment building on New York's Fifth Avenue, overlooking Central Park. This was a rare event, according to ornithologists, because hawks don't usually take kindly to an urban environment. Anyhow, a small group of bird-watchers set up camp across the street and, armed with binoculars, kept track of the domestic habits of these latest arrivals to the high-rent district. In no time, they developed a close-knit community brought together by a common interest. They chatted and gossiped. They shared hot chocolate to ward off the morning chill, and more potent potables when happy hour rolled around. They kept track of the types of twigs, branches, and straw used by the hawks to construct their nest. They noted how long Mama Hawk sat on her nest, and how many times and for how long she was relieved of her duties by her (presumably) liberated mate.

But all was not at ease in Zion. As in any good soap, there were several concurrent stories going on. One of these had to do with rodents—field mice, to be exact. They had become a nuisance in the Park, and the City of New York decided upon mass extermination, which would involve putting poison in the burrows where the mice made their homes. Now to hawks, field mice are considered a delicacy, and if Papa Hawk were to take a piece of the flesh of a poisoned rodent to the nest, he or Mama Hawk might inadvertently serve up a lethal breakfast to their helpless young. And so when the bird-watchers got wind of the city's plan, they were exceeding wroth; they circulated a petition, engaged competent

· · · · · ·

110

counsel, and soon were successful in obtaining a court-ordered injunction against the extermination. Thank God, the Hawk family would be saved!

Now what is wrong with this picture? Well, in reading the article, I couldn't help wondering if the same indignant citizens would have been moved to get a court-ordered injunction against the absentee Harlem landlord two miles to the north of the Hawk family's apartment building, in order to prevent *human* babies from being bitten by the more unpleasant kind of rodents that infest tenements. With all due respect to animals, and "all creatures great and small," I must go on record saying that the story suggested to me the kind of misplaced values, and misplaced compassion—and passion—of so many in our midst today. Is it my imagination, or has the press made the advocacy of whales, bison, bald eagles, and dolphins more popular and more fashionable than providing, for example, for those whom Jesus called "the least of these my brethren"?

In the parable of the unjust steward (Luke 16), Jesus told his hearers that the children of this world are wiser than the children of light. What he meant was that people with a cause are more focused, more intentional in doing their thing than Christians are in doing theirs. He may well have had our Fifth Avenue bird-watchers in mind. Maybe we should take a page from their book. It seems to me that if we were as zealous about the Gospel as they are about the plight of unborn hawks, we could work miracles. We could, with Jesus, preach the good news to the poor, proclaim release to the captives, and set at liberty those who are oppressed.

> *Every task, however simple, sets the soul that does it free;*
> *every deed of human kindness done in love is done to thee.*
> *Jesus, thou divine Companion, help us all to work our best;*
> *bless us in our daily labor, lead us to our Sabbath rest.*

Henry Van Dyke, "Jesus thou Divine Companion," *The Hymnal 1982*, No. 586

"I dare not trust the sweetest frame, but wholly lean on Jesus' Name"

—Lift Every Voice and Sing II, No. 99

AT CAESAREA PHILIPPI, there is an identity crisis of sorts. Jesus asks his disciples, who have been following him for several months, what people are saying about him. The answers come in rapid succession. Like many of us, they were experts on other people's opinions and behavior. They tell Jesus that some say he is John the Baptist, others Elijah, others one of the prophets. But when Jesus asks them point blank who *they* think he is, they are not so forthcoming. After an awkward silence, the impetuous Peter blurts out, "Thou art the Christ, the son of the living God."

The good news is that the great Petrine Confession is a pivotal event in the Gospel. The bad news is that as Jesus spells out what Messiahship means—when he tells the disciples that he would have to undergo suffering and be put to death—Peter takes exception and actually pulls Jesus aside and upbraids him! Like so many of us, Peter wants to fashion a Jesus born of his own "druthers." We make Jesus a meek and mild Savior or a voice for the so-called silent majority; or we make him into a homophobe or a racist, to suit our own needs, often choosing to ignore what the Bible says about Jesus and what he says about himself. We balk, too, at the suggestion that we must pick up our cross and follow him.

Perhaps the emperor Constantine did us a disservice. We are told that early in the fourth century, he looked up to the sky and saw a cross, under which was written "*In hoc signo vinces*" (In this sign shalt thou conquer). He took this as a sign that he should convert to Christianity, and when he did, the church, previously underground (sometimes literally), became "official." You could no longer be martyred for your beliefs. Christianity had become respectable. A question we might ask ourselves is: if Christianity were still illegal,

. . . . . .

and we were arrested, would there be enough evidence to convict us?

The renowned preacher Herbert O'Driscoll writes of a visit to a mall with his grandson during which he realized that the postmodern world of his children's children defines everybody primarily as consumers. What a long way, he thought, from his Irish youth, when, if asked, he would have described himself as a child of God and an inheritor of the kingdom of heaven. Our religious identity, along with our racial, sexual, and nationalistic identities, tends to be fluid nowadays. *USA Today* reported a poll in which the majority of respondents described themselves as "spiritual but not religious." "Brand loyalty" is less of a factor for those GenX folk seeking church affiliation. Geographical proximity, the Christian education program, or the non-traditional services offered by the congregation (such as fitness classes and investment clubs) are likely to loom large in the decision-making process.

When asked to say who people say we are, our prayer is that we may answer with conviction in the words of a great evangelical hymn:

> *My hope is built on nothing less*
> *Than Jesus' blood and righteousness.*
> *I dare not trust the sweetest frame,*
> *But wholly lean on Jesus' name.*
> > *On Christ, the solid Rock, I stand,*
> > *All other ground is sinking sand.*

Edward Mote, "On Christ, the solid Rock, I stand," *Lift Every Voice and Sing II*, No. 99

"Brand us this day with Jesus' Name"

—The Hymnal 1982, No. 297

THERE IS A STORY told about an English missionary sent to serve in a parish in the then Diocese of British Guyana in the Province of the West Indies. One of his first official acts was to preside at Baptism on Easter Even, at which there were some twenty or so candidates. It had long been the custom in that parish for mothers to pin the name of the child on the inside hem of the baptismal gown so as to ensure that the officiant would give each child his or her rightful name. The new priest was not aware of the custom, and so, when the first child was handed to him, he solemnly made the request in the words prescribed in the Prayer Book: "Name this child." The godmother, in an attempt to acquaint the vicar with the local practice, responded, "Pinned upon she." The missionary, doubtless lamenting that Christian names had fallen into desuetude, dipped the silver shell into the font, and poured the water over the infant's head, saying, "Pinda Ponshee, I baptize you in the Name of the Father, and of the Son, and of the Holy Ghost."

Unfortunately, too many Episcopalians—like the good vicar—have taken lately to bestowing careless names upon one another. Persons who describe themselves as traditionalist and orthodox are dismissed as conservative and fundamentalist. Self-proclaimed liberals are called secular humanists by their detractors. Those who hold to a belief in biblical inerrancy describe those who espouse a different brand of exegesis as revisionists. Even epithets like "heretic" and "apostate" are being hurled at fellow Christians with what we used to call gay abandon. Gone are the days when there were basically only three camps within the church—low and lazy, broad and hazy, high and crazy—all of which fit easily under the umbrella of Anglicanism. Nowadays, Episcopalians want to share their refuge only with those who are exactly like-minded; everybody else is sent out into the rain.

. . . . . .

It is both ironic and tragic that in an age in which so much progress has been made in the interfaith dialogue, there seems to be more infighting within the Christian denominations. In this new century, Anglicans, especially, need to rediscover the *via media*. They should be instructed, perhaps, by the genius of the compilers of the 1789 Book of Common Prayer, who sought "to keep the happy mean between too much stiffness in refusing, and too much easiness in admitting variations in things once advisedly established." In other words, opposing groups must be willing to eschew, on the one hand, a "stiffness" in which tradition becomes "a solid rock from the dead past" and avoid, on the other hand, an "easiness" in which we become "tossed to and fro with every vain blast of doctrine." Then they might see that there is room under the umbrella for all sorts and conditions of men and women.

> *Descend, O Spirit, purging flame,*
> *brand us this day with Jesus' Name!*
> *Confirm our faith, consume our doubt;*
> *sign us as Christ's, within, without.*

Scott Francis Brenner, "Descend, O Spirit, purging flame," *The Hymnal 1982*, No. 297

> *"Grant us wisdom, grant us courage, lest we miss thy kingdom's goal"*
> —*The Hymnal 1982*, No. 594

WE OFTEN HEAR ABOUT PEOPLE "finding" themselves. The child of a friend or colleague, after having some difficulty adjusting to the rigors of college life, for example, takes a year off "to find himself." People find themselves by getting in touch with their inner self, their spirituality, or the side of the brain they haven't been using. Finding oneself is akin to getting one's act together, discovering one's niche in life, or, like Stella, in a recent hit movie, getting one's groove back! It's all about self-realization, becoming a "better" person. I think it is related to what psychologists call differentiation, the process of establishing one's unique identity in relationship to everybody else's.

I'm afraid this is not what Jesus had in mind. Our clue to understanding what Jesus meant can, in fact, be found in the parable of the prodigal son. When he found himself, when he "came to himself," (and the moment of self-discovery was when he was on the skids, when he was forced to feed swine, the ultimate degradation for a Jew) he returned home—to God. Finding oneself, as Jesus means it, has to do, not with uncovering some sense of inner satisfaction, but with discovering oneself in light of God's plan. It has to do with responding to a higher calling, and for that reason, it actually necessitates losing, rather than finding, oneself. Jesus said: "Whoever would save his life will lose it, and whoever loses his life for my sake and the gospel's will save it. For what shall it profit a man if he shall gain the whole world, and lose his soul?" (Mark 8:35–36)

Much as we buy into the self-actualization mode of finding ourselves, we know that true satisfaction comes when we empty ourselves to be of service to others. This is what ministry—lay and ordained—is all about: coming to serve and not to be served. And, if I may mount my hobbyhorse for a minute, I believe that the church will be better served when those seeking ordination realize that ministry is about service and not, ultimately, self-fulfillment. The church will be better off when her prospective clergy proclaim, with Isaiah, "Here I am, send me," and not, as many do, "Here I am, and this is where I am willing to go."

Ministry aside, we know that, when money is hoarded, it is lost. The parable of the talents—and our financial advisors—tell us that. When we hoard our health, it becomes hypochondria. When we clutch onto our lives, we become obsessed with drawing breath and a paycheck, and not with "having life and having it abundantly."

> *Cure thy children's warring madness,*
> *bend our pride to thy control;*
> *shame our wanton, selfish gladness,*
> *rich in things and poor in soul.*
> *Grant us wisdom, grant us courage,*
> *lest we miss thy kingdom's goal.*
>
> Harry Emerson Fosdick, "God of grace and God of glory," *The Hymnal 1982*, No. 594

THAT UNSAVORY NEIGHBORHOOD called "Outer Darkness" in the Gospel of Matthew is a rather crowded place. The hapless wedding guest wearing the wrong clothes (Matthew 22:13) was sent there, and so was the servant who beat up his fellow servants and caroused with his low-life friends (Matthew 24:49–51). Later, those guys are joined by the "one-talent man" (Matthew 25:30). He was the one, who, afraid of taking a risk, hid his talent in the ground, while his friends' investments yielded a hundred percent return. The one-talent man's unwillingness to take a risk caused his master to call him "wicked and slothful." It was because he decided to play it safe that the Lord took away what he had and gave it to the other guys.

Churches have their share of one-talent Christians. There are those who mouth the seven deadly words: "We have always done it that way." There are others who hoard their treasure and share very little of it. There are others who want the church to play it safe, to say nothing to the world or even to each other about the issues that affect our lives every day. To take no risk on matters having to do with our faith is really to make a non-commitment by default. Archbishop Desmond Tutu, in a not-too-veiled reference to the church's role in the dismantling of apartheid, is fond of telling the story of the mouse and the elephant. A mouse finds himself immobilized because an elephant has just sat down on the poor little creature's tail. He tries in escape, but to no avail. Then the king of the jungle happens by, and the mouse sees his opportunity. He entreats him: "Mr. Lion, if you would be kind enough to let out a great roar, the elephant will be frightened and will run away, and I can be free." The lion responds, "I am sorry to hear about your plight, Mr. Mouse, but I hasten to point out that whatever is going on is a matter between you and Mr. Elephant, and does not concern me in the least." "Do as you wish," replies the desperate mouse, but may *I* hasten to point out that either you are part of the problem or part of the solution?"

> *Awake, my soul, stretch every nerve,*
>   *and press with vigor on;*
> *a heavenly race demands thy zeal,*
>   *and an immortal crown.*
>
> *'tis God's all-animating voice*
>   *that calls thee from on high;*
> *'tis his own hand presents the prize*
>   *to thine inspiring eye.*
>
> Philip Doddridge, "Awake, my soul, stretch every nerve," *The Hymnal 1982*, No. 546

> *"Breathe on me, Breath of God, so shall I never die"*
>
> —*The Hymnal 1982*, No. 508

TWO DAYS AFTER a fatal Amtrak derailment a few years ago, the media moved their focus from the facts of the case to what they refer to as "human interest." I turned on the morning news, and found that the parents of two of the victims were being interviewed. Two of their three daughters had lost their lives in the collision between their passenger train and a speeding truck. I sat, my morning routine suspended, listening, as a very handsome and, from all appearances, well-heeled couple from Mississippi sat in front of oil paintings of their daughters, and recounted the awful events of that split second which had changed their lives forever.

But what made their testimony so riveting is that they said that their faith had seen them through the catastrophe. They told the viewing public that their faith in Jesus Christ and the prayers and support of their family and friends had sustained them. The girls' mother said that when she saw the sleeping car engulfed in flames, the only thing that kept her from hysteria was the knowledge that her children were safe in the arms of Jesus. And then, their father recounted that just the previous week, as he was driving his girls to school, the Lord, for reasons he did not understand at the time, had laid it on his heart to talk to them about salvation, and what heaven was like. As if that weren't enough, the bereft father said of the truck driver: "We all make mistakes," and proceeded to say "we forgive him. We shudder to think how much is going through his mind this morning; it will not help him to add to his pain by heaping more guilt on his shoulders." Then they thanked the reporter for allowing them to tell their whole story, since other networks had edited out all references to their faith. The viewing public, presumably, would rather see devastated, desolate, dejected victims, shaking their fists at God, crying "Why me?" and vowing to avenge their children's deaths. Despair, presumably, sells more newspapers than hope.

. . . . . .

Death and hope are placed in juxtaposition in the story of the raising of Lazarus, which teaches us something about both. In it, we learn that we all die. Perhaps there is nothing that causes us to be in denial more than this fact. Our language betrays us. In one homiletics class I taught, one of my students began a sermon on the rich man and Lazarus by saying "The rich man passed away." I suggested to him that if St. Luke wrote "the rich man died," then we would do well not to improve on the original with "passed away" or any of the other euphemisms: "passed on"; "is in a better place"; "is no longer with us"; "breathed one's last"; or simply "is gone."

The evangelist goes to pains to show that Lazarus is in fact dead, not merely resting or sleeping. Martha knows this. Martha, the fastidious one who busied herself whipping up soufflés every time Jesus visited, feels she has to warn Jesus: "By this time, Lord, there will be an odor, for he has been dead four days." Or in the blunt language of the King James Version, "by now he stinketh."

Having established death, the evangelist then moves toward hope. Jesus approaches Lazarus' grave and says, "Lazarus, come out." And Lazarus steps forth, still enveloped in his burial cloths. Then Jesus orders: "Unbind him and let him go." And Lazarus, once dead, now lives. The people see the glory of God. Mary and Martha get their brother back. Everybody's happy. Curtain. It's a wrap!

But wait, there's more! There is more to our faith than hanging around waiting to die so that we can share in the joy of the Resurrection. Christianity is not a heavenly insurance policy whose premiums are church-going, living a good life, and being kind to neighbors. Jesus said we shall have life and have it abundantly, and that means sharing in the joy of the Resurrection every day. As Ezekiel reminds us, our lives can often be like a pile of dry bones. Who among us hasn't cried to God, at one time or another, "Our bones are dried up and our hope is lost. We are cut off completely." The sad fact is we don't have to wait until we "breathe our last" in order to die. We speak of marriages and other relationships that have died. In some places, we speak of churches that our dead. When this is the case, like Ezekiel, we ask that the breath of God will come and breathe new life into those dry bones.

If we are honest, we admit that we experience little deaths all the time. Severe depression deadens our spirit. Addictive and compulsive behaviors kill our spirit long before they kill our bodies. And when this happens, our prayer is that our Lord will free us from such bonds just as he freed Lazarus from the bonds of death: "Unbind him and let him go."

If we but listen, we will learn something from that couple in Mississippi. Our faith is not merely a set of doctrines to which we give intellectual assent. Nor is it just a series of ceremonies in which we participate to mark rites of passage—the "hatch, match, and dispatch" approach. And it certainly is not something designed to give respectability to our lives. Our faith is a tool, a resource, that not only gives meaning to life, but enables us, in good times and in bad, to cope, to understand, to find a way when there is no way, to have life and to have it abundantly.

> *Breathe on me, Breath of God,*
> *fill me with life anew,*
> *that I may love what thou dost love,*
> *and do what thou wouldst do.*
>
> *Breathe on me, Breath of God,*
> *so shall I never die;*
> *but live with thee the perfect life*
> *of thine eternity.*

> Edwin Hatch, "Breath on me, Breath of God," *The Hymnal 1982*, No. 508